WHAT MAKES PEOPLE BORING?

ARVIND UPADHYAY

ISBN 979-888521386-8

Why? Basically, humans tend to fall into a serious habit of doing the same thing repeatedly. You could even say that a part of us is designed to be boring.

Here's what I mean. It's a natural instinct for us to not spend our energy making conscious active decisions throughout the day. In fact, we make about 35,000 decisions per day on autopilot. They take place in our basal ganglia instead of the prefrontal cortex.

The reason is, we were built to reserve our energy for fight-or-flight mode to survive in the wild. What's more, we're designed to procrastinate to avoid any stressors in life.

The glaring problem? We're not living out in the wild anymore (most of us anyway, particularly if you're reading this article from your computer).

So, if our species is designed to reserve energy and procrastinate on those adventurous plans you dream about, imagine doing that for decades. Put another way, the longer you repeat your boring habits the more stuck you become in those habits.And when you're stuck in a habit of doing the same thing repeatedly (for decades), you're more susceptible to other outcomes that make you even more boring.

Contents

Foreword

Every Wednesday is Tip Day.

This Wednesday: Seven tips for knowing if you're boring someone.

In one of my favorite movies, a quirky documentary called Sherman's March, the documentary maker's former high school teacher tells him, "As people get older, they get more like themselves. And you're getting more boring." I've never forgotten that.

Like most people, probably, I have several pet subjects that I love to talk about – subjects that are sometimes interesting to other people, and sometimes not. Don't get me started on happiness, or obesity, or children's literature, or Winston Churchill, unless you really want to talk about it. (I do manage to be very disciplined about not talking about my children too much.)

I've developed a list of signs to look for, as indicators that I might be boring someone. Just because a person isn't actually walking away or changing the subject doesn't mean that that person is genuinely engaged in a conversation. One challenge is that the more socially adept a person is, the better he or she is at hiding boredom. It's a rare person, however, who can truly look fascinated while stifling a yawn.

Here are the factors I watch, when trying to figure out if I'm connecting with someone. These are utterly unscientific – I'm sure someone has made a proper study of this, but these are just my observations (mostly from noting how I behave when I'm bored and trying to hide it):

1. Repeated, perfunctory responses. A person who says, "Oh really? Oh really? That's interesting. Oh really?" is probably not too engaged.

2. Simple questions. People who are bored ask simple questions. "When did you move?" "Where did you go?" People who are interested ask more complicated questions that show curiosity, not mere politeness.

3. Interruption. Although it sounds rude, interruption is actually a good sign, I think. It means a person is bursting to say something, and that shows interest. Similiarly...

4. Request for clarification. A person who is sincerely interested in what you're saying will need you to elaborate or to explain. "What does that term mean?" "When exactly did that happen?" "Back up and tell me what happened first" are the kinds of questions that show that someone is trying closely to follow what you're saying.

5. Imbalance of talking time. I suspect that many people fondly suppose that they usually do eighty percent of the talking in a conversation because people find them fascinating. Sometimes, it's true, a discussion involves a huge download of information desired by the listener; that's a very satisfying kind of conversation. In general, though, people who are interested in a subject have things to say themselves; they want to add their own opinions, information, and experiences. If they aren't doing that, they probably just want the conversation to end faster.

6. Body position. People with a good connection generally turn fully to face each other. A person who is partially turned away isn't fully embracing the conversation.

Along the same lines, if you're a speaker trying to figure out if an audience is interested in what you're saying:

7. Audience posture. Back in 1885, Sir Francis Galton wrote a paper in 1885 called "The Measurement of Fidget." He determined that people slouch and lean when bored, so a speaker can measure the boredom of an audience by seeing how far from vertically upright they are. Also, attentive people fidget less; bored people fidget more. An audience that's upright and still is interested, while an audience that's horizontal and squirmy is bored.

I often remind myself of La Rochefoucauld's observation, "We are always bored by those whom we bore." If I'm bored, there's a good chance the other person may be bored, too. Time to find a different subject.

Have you figured out any ways to tell if you're boring someone?

*

Preface

Everything is boring sometimes because you are not being challenged enough by your studies or work, and other times it may be because of your emotional state.

There are many reasons why everything is boring all of a sudden and you can change how you approach new challenges to get rid of this feeling.

If you suddenly feel like everything is boring, there may be many reasons behind it and you may want to find out what is applicable to you, so you can do something about it.Everything may seem boring because you are depressed, or maybe you are just not doing what you are really interested in. Here are some other reasons why everything is boring to you these days.

Maybe you find everything boring because you are not socializing enough.

During this epidemic a lot of people have felt the sensation that everything is boring, and when everything feels boring people may have a tendency to cut the social life of any kind of their life.

While people cannot meet in person right now, there has been a definite rise in social media use, and you can still hang out with your friends virtually and talk to them on video or phone calls.

If you want things to be more exciting and for everything to not be boring, you'll have to make the effort to invite people into your life.

While you may feel like not seeing anyone right now, once you make the effort to see your friends you might feel a lot better.

A huge reason why suddenly everything is boring maybe because you are depressed.

Depression can make enjoyable activities boring and your experience of pleasure in those activities can decrease substantially, leading you to feel like you are bored.

Another reason depression makes everything seem boring is that it causes a loss of motivation, which in turn keeps you from accomplishing things like you used to.

In addition to the constant sadness that comes with depression, it can also make the patient feel like everything is boring due to a lack of pleasure in anything

Food may taste bland, sleep is not restful anymore, and as a consequence, the brain tends to get sort of numb, and this removes emotion from a lot of days to day things that might have seemed interesting in other circumstances.

Depression may make the person feel tired and listless all day, so when it comes to doing things that may not seem boring, they don't have the energy to do it, and so everything is boring all the time.

Your mind can think that everything is boring if you are an adult with sexual needs that have not been met in a long time.

Sex is a primal need that human beings have, and when they are deprived of that for too long, it can start to feel like everything is mundane and boring.

Sex is one of the important, basic needs like food, water, shelter, and comfort, due to its evolutionary importance.

When sex is suddenly removed from the equation for a long time it can seem like everything is pointless and boring.

Furthermore, sex brings about the release of pleasure related hormones, and this causes things to be interesting and lessens the feeling that everything is boring.

When someone's entire reproductive system, which happens to be a primary motivation for so many of a human being's actions is not being satiated.

When you let yourself go, so to speak, and start to ignore your mental and physical health, and stop making the effort to be productive every day, it can seem like everything is boring.

It has been seen often, especially during this epidemic quarantine, that many people have stopped doing the things that make them feel like themselves, like dressing a certain way.

Now many people are stuck feeling like someone else, because of this new forced routine, and it's wearing on everyone, making it seem like everything is boring.

When someone has not invigorated themselves in a long time, it can severely hamper their creativity, but it can also be remedied by the people themselves, which is the great part.

When you are stuck in the same physical place forever, like in this epidemic situation, it can seem like everything is boring, because you have been looking at the same thing forever.

While there is not much you can do about it, it does explain why you may feel that everything is boring. Human beings are not built for an isolated, cooped up lifestyle, and it can have an adverse effect on anyone's mind.

It may be hard to read but a reason everything is boring is maybe because you have become a boring, different version of yourself.

Sometimes when we have been in a rut for some time, we tend to start being routine and mundane ourselves.

In this case, when you have stopped trying to do new things or trying new activities, it may seem like everything is boring, but really it is just a function of the fact that you just are not trying hard enough to find newness and interesting things anymore.

Maybe you are feeling bored because you keep saying "No" to things you could be saying, "Yes!" to, so now you find yourself having nothing to talk or even recall in your free moments.

Sometimes things seem boring because you are not able to achieve Flow in whatever you are doing.

Flow is a state of total concentration and being totally involved in the task you are currently doing, which is at the same time challenging and yet close to one's capabilities.

In colloquial language Flow may be compared to the phrase "being in the zone".

Flow occurs when someone's skills match the level of challenge they take on and when a task includes clear goals and immediate feedback.

Too easy tasks are boring; too difficult to make your attention wander and break the flow.

For optimum engagement in a task at hand it needs to match the person's skill and interest level.

When you engage in such tasks and achieve complete flow things do no seem quite so boring anymore because you are deeply involved.

Feeling like everything is boring may be linked to problems with attention.

People who suffer from attention deficit hyperactivity disorder are a good example of this theory.

They tend to move from task to task without ever completing any one of them with success, because their attention tends to wander, and they get bored.

At the same time when we are bored, we never engage our attention.

This creates a cycle, you are bored, your attention wanders, things feel even more boring.

If you often feel like you are bored and this keeps you from performing properly, you should explore the idea with your doctor that you may have attentional problems.

People who lack self-awareness, especially about their emotions and feelings tend to be prone to boredom.

This may also be due to the fact that a bored individual is not able to articulate properly what they want to do.

When someone has trouble describing what they feel or what they want to do, they may feel like everything is boring and they can't find anything interesting to do.

To stop feeling like everything is boring first you need to figure out why you feel that everything is boring.

Once you know why you feel this way it will be easier to figure out what to do about it.

When you complain over and over that everything is boring, you tend to forget why you started feeling that way in the first place.

When you list the causes of why you feel that everything is boring, you might actually end up finding a solution to the boredom.

Other tips to stop feeling that everything is boring are:

· Do something you are afraid of. Fear can motivate you immensely and doing something you are afraid of can stimulate your mind because you are more aware of everything around you

· Stop doing what you are doing when you feel like everything is boring. Once you do that do the exact opposite of what you were doing, hopefully, something that involves all your senses. Listen to loud music, look at colorful images, go find everything you can smell, and engage all parts of your brain.

· Take rest. It may be that you are feeling that everything is boring because you are too tired and fatigue has set into your mind making everything seem duller.

· Keep going forward and trying new things whether you succeed at them or not. This can eventually remind you that challenges are fun and take away the boredom.

If everything is boring when you are sober, you may want to consider that you may have been spending too much time under the influence of substances, and your brain may have gotten far too used to being hyped up on alcohol or drugs.

Many people start feeling like everything is boring when they are sober when they are constantly used to the situations of partying and having many people around all the time, which is why when that stimulation goes away you are not able to cope well.

Also, if you have been taking substances that are stimulating, like marijuana or amphetamines, everything can seem even more boring when you are sober, and you need to consider getting help for this feeling because this is what might often turn into addiction because might keep going back to substances to get rid of the feeling of boring.

If everything is boring when you are sober, you may try the following tips:

Find a hobby that is stimulating to your mind

Find a new workout regimen

Hang out with a group of people that don't like substances

Find newer ways to fill your time

Don't spend too much time alone.

Everything is boring, What should I do?

If you feel like everything is boring, here are some things you should do:

Talk to your friends

Find new hobbies

Find alternate work

Find ways to engage your mind in the work you are currently doing

Go to bed and wake up at a regular time

See a counselor or psychologist

If everything is boring, you should find new challenges, because often it can simply be a lack of challenge that is making you feel bored and odd, because lacking flow in things you do can be a huge reason for feeling bored and not enjoying anything anymore.

If you keep feeling like everything is boring, you might also need to look at what activities you enjoy, and find related activities that may help you pass the time.

Furthermore, when everything is boring, you should make sure you are not experiencing other symptoms that might signal the possibility of depression or anxiety, because not being able to experience pleasure or engagement in things you do can often be a sign of poor mental health as well.

CHAPTER ONE

I'm in Love and It's Really Boring

The best kind of love is the boring kind.

We grow up thinking love is frenzied. Rabid. Raving. A movie reel of running into water holding hands and rapid making out and biting lips and hot feelings and mascara and late nights and early mornings sipping coffee talking about the future in long, desperate threads of passion.

If you need an example, I wrote the following in my diary when I was seventeen:

"Kyle Knox [name changed to protect, let's be honest, myself] left me a comment on MySpace the other day. I haven't talked to that boy for a year. And he is the hottest boy on the planet still here to this day. I miss him. I really do. I miss sitting in class and starring at every move he makes. It's the only sense of entertainment I got during the whole entire school day there. And it was amazing. I wish we were madly in love. Can't get enough of each other love."

Print by Megan Galante

The best kind of love is the boring kind.

We grow up thinking love is frenzied. Rabid. Raving. A movie reel of running into water holding hands and rapid making out and biting lips and hot feelings and mascara and late nights and early mornings sipping coffee talking about the future in long, desperate threads of passion.

If you need an example, I wrote the following in my diary when I was seventeen:

"Kyle Knox [name changed to protect, let's be honest, myself] left me a comment on MySpace the other day. I haven't talked to that boy for a year. And he is the hottest boy on the planet still here to this day. I miss him. I really do. I miss sitting in class and starring at every move he makes. It's the only sense of entertainment I got during the whole entire school day there. And it was amazing. I wish we were madly in love. Can't get enough of each other love."

High School was a rage storm of connecting dots and encoding relationships. I talked about nothing but boys. Pages and pages and pages were dedicated to prom alone. I imagined falling for someone deeply, like trust falling into a waterfall. I expected feverish love to happen like the snap of a finger: "CRACK! You're exquisitely in denial of ever loving yourself as much as you love another human! Much congrats!"

Of course, relationships don't work that way. They take the work. They take the openness and patience and silence. The work doesn't need to be erratic and packed tight with short extremes of hot and cold. The work takes time. The work can be boring. It can be warm.

My love is all of those things. It takes the work. And dammit, it's a boring, beautiful thing.

I got engaged in May. We had been together for six years. We drove down the coast from Portland to San Diego. He asked me on the balcony of our hotel, while we were sipping Ballast Point and I was reading him snippets from my road notebook. The moment was perfectly us. We were alone. The engagement wasn't a spectacle. And I cried so hard in happiness, I thought he was going to change his mind. Afterwards, we ate crappy pizza in the Gaslamp District and stared at the ring and chuckled at each other under fluorescent lights. "Now, what do we do?" I remember asking him at some point in the night, and he looked at me and laughed, "Pay off that thing."

I can't pinpoint the exact moment we fell in love. To me, our moments fused together, the small fragments of their picture a stitch. One day the moments needled an entire blanket, suddenly warm enough to cover both of us. Joan Didion wrote in A Year of Magical Thinking that she didn't believe in the general notion of falling in love. She simply knew when she wanted to have someone near her; spend her life with that person. So, maybe love is a timing thing. Maybe love is about space. The right kind of "love" is so constant and stable and simple, a wordsmith and spirit like Didion finds its effortlessness difficult to define.

Passion fades. Spontaneity can get us in trouble. Constantly asking "What should we do next?" will pill a relationship like any bad sweater rubbing against your pits. Good love is boring. Good love is sitting in silence after work on a Tuesday, elbow-to-elbow at a stale dive bar watching a

Celebrity Bowling Championship sharing a pizza, finding comfort in car rides because you listen to good music loudly and he tries to rap and you laugh with him. These moments are stable and reliable. They're secure. They're boring.

One thing I really love about my fiancé is that he's very comfortable in this kind of love. (Writer's Note: Calling him fiancé is super weird to me and kind of sounds pompous? The word is perfectly complimentary of a middle finger proving to everyone else that you've fallen in love. No? Anyway.) He doesn't expect me to be his bombastic lover. He expects me to be me—sweatpants and a Pete Hamill novel with the slippers I can microwave so their lavender beans can warm my toes throughout the winter. Of course I can surprise him here or there, but he's happy when I'm doing my thing. And he's even happier when he's doing his thing.

My favorite example of this happened right in the beginning of our relationship. My love language is "physical touch" and his is "acts of service." He'd rather start my car in the morning than spoon me for hours on end. Despite that, we still cuddle. One day during a cuddle session, he rolled over to get up for the bathroom. I pouted a little bit at the blank spot on the bed and he said, "Brittany, you need to fight your own battles now." It made me laugh; now looking back, I realized how right he was. Even if he wasn't trying to make a point.

It isn't anyone else's responsibility to keep me entertained. That's my damn prerogative! Also, it's not my fiancé's responsibility to give me constant romantic hedonism—we'll leave that to the Bachelor. Grandiose declarations of love and travel and gifts should not be love's expectation. Love's expectation should be respect, and their time...listening, sharing stories, being quiet, support, making coffee for them in the morning, folding the towels, taking out the garbage. The boring stuff.

I'm not saying you can't have any surprises in a relationship. Or to remain completely quiet. We argue. I have my opinion. He has his. We have stupid moments where we should have thought through a decision together a little differently. But we find ways to sprinkle excitement into our relationship, too. I'm not saying that's not important.

Being boring gives the bigger moments in a relationship even more gusto. When we do decide to take a trip, we're dazzled by what a new place gives us. We watch the world in an entirely new way together. We're enlightened and happy, thankful to take a break in the mundane. These moments are so powerful against the grey backdrop of everyday life—travel makes us better, more grateful, closer to home.

The best kind of love is the boring kind. It has to be. It's meant to be.

REAL LOVE...IT'S NOT A GAME YOU DON'T UNDERSTAND THE RULES OF, OR A TEST YOU NEVER GOT THE MATERIALS TO STUDY FOR. IT NEVER LEAVES YOU WONDERING...WHAT YOU COULD POSSIBLY DO TO MAKE IT COME HOME AND STAY THERE. IT'S FUCKING BORING, DUDE. I DON'T WALK AROUND MIRED IN UNEASINESS, WAITING FOR THE OTHER SHOE TO DROP...THIS FEELS SAFE AND STEADFAST AND PREDICTABLE AND SECURE. IT'S BORING AS SHIT. AND IT'S EASILY THE BEST THING I'VE EVER FELT.

Relationships can become boring, especially if both partners have started putting less effort into trying to enjoy each other and joint activities. However, being bored doesn't sound like the biggest of problems and that is precisely why it can become a serious issue.

Boredom is among the most common reasons behind failing relationships, alongside severe emotional distancing between partners, problems with dishonesty in a relationship, and losing attraction to your significant other. This is why it is important to address relationship boredom as soon as you notice this issue.

There are many reasons behind your relationship getting a bit stale, and it is important to identify the root cause in order to start resolving the issue. If you find it difficult to rekindle the joyful spark, an experienced coach can provide professional emotional intimacy coaching that can help you and your partner find excitement again. However, it's important to understand the reason behind this problem and its possible effects.

Is It Normal To Be Bored In A Relationship?

People feel bored all the time and relationships are no exceptions. However, experiencing relationship boredom can feel especially discouraging because it can make you question you and your partner's compatibility and potential for a lasting loving relationship.

All that said, being bored in a relationship is a normal and common issue that happens to many couples. However, that doesn't mean that you don't need to do anything to alleviate the situation and let it unfold on its own. As usual and as frequent boredom in a relationship might be, it is something to pay attention to and attempt to resolve.

Relationship boredom can be a sign of a more serious underlying problem or it can lead to serious relationship issues if left unresolved. That is why it's important to understand why you're experiencing relationship boredom and consider implementing methods to deal with it in a healthy, constructive way.

Why Does A Relationship Become Boring?

There are many reasons why relationships can become boring. Discovering and pinpointing the reasons behind the feelings of boredom can greatly help improve your relationship with your partner. Here are some of the most common reasons why couples can go through a period of stagnation:

Going with the flow

It's easy to become overly comfortable in a relationship, and that's not a bad thing. However, it can start posing problems if it leads to long periods of uneventfulness.

Always going on the beaten path

Some couples find the things they love doing together and then stick to them all the time. It can be very beneficial for relationships to spice things up once in a while.

Forgetting about yourself

Some individuals lose themselves in relationships, which can cause them to lose their own goals in life, leading to individual boredom that gets transferred to the entire relationship.

Not working on physical intimacy

It's easy for sexual encounters to become means to an orgasmic end in relationships. This can lead to a dissatisfying sexual life, which can only enhance the feeling of boredom.

Neglecting emotional intimacy

Emotional intimacy is just as important as physical intimacy, and relationship stagnation can often be caused by a partner's inability or unwillingness to share their emotions.

Not sharing hobbies

Sometimes, relationship boredom can be caused by not having enough activities to share with your partner.

Never having arguments

Constantly arguing with your partner can be extremely detrimental to a relationship, but so can complacency and constant compromising. It can be healthy to share diverging opinions from time to time and allow both yourself and your partner to express different points of view.

Do Couples Get Tired Of Each Other?

Looking around you, it might be easy to notice couples and spouses who are tired of each other and think of it as an inevitability of life. However, there is no emotional or psychological rule that states that all couples get tired of each other and that there is nothing you can do about it besides waiting for it to happen to you.

The truth is that the majority of couples go through rough patches and experience problems in the relationship. However, the lack of taking action, to resolve the problems that arise, is often the reason behind unhappy or unsuccessful relationships.

So, although some couples do "get tired of each other" and relationship boredom may arise from time to time, that doesn't immediately mean that your relationship is at its end. Many relationship issues require active involvement, not quitting.

How Do I Fix My Boredom In A Relationship?

If you're willing to work on and through the feelings of boredom in your relationship, there are several things you can try doing to break up the habit and inspire enthusiasm and excitement:

Be honest with your partner about what's going on and work on it together.

Find a way to break up the same old daily routine and spice things up.

Try surprising your partner and making the relationship more dynamic.

Consider changing your current environment since this can also help with eliminating boredom.

Create a bucket list for your relationship consisting of all the things you'd like to do together.

Start touching your partner more and show them how you feel through physical intimacy.

Go on dates and remember the feeling of first meeting each other.

Start flirting with your partner again and revive the lost spark.

Consider taking up a new hobby together.

However, you have to be aware of the fact that sometimes, even against you and your partner's best efforts, boredom will not seem to go away. At these times, you might want to consider truing professional emotional coaching. Experienced relationship advocates can help you find the underlying problem behind this issue and change behavioral patterns that might be the cause.

Start Rebuilding Intimacy In Your Relationship At PIVOT

Although experiencing boredom in a relationship does not sound like the most serious problem couples can face, it is still a matter that requires your attention. Being in a boring relationship may cause serious relationship challenges and even breakups.

However, it is never too late to reconnect with your partner and rediscover the joy and the excitement you once had. Even if you struggle to do it alone, you can always turn to qualified relationship coaches for professional emotional intimacy coaching that will help you with building intimacy and interest in your relationship again.

Every relationship has its ups and downs. The early stages are often marked by intense and passionate emotions that gradually temper with time. As your relationship grows steadier and more comfortable, you might start to fear that it is growing a bit too well-worn—or even a little boring.

Your relationship might be mostly free of conflict, but you still might find yourself feeling unsatisfied, tired, or just plain uninspired. So can you inject some excitement back into a monotonous relationship, or is it time to move on and find a fresh start?

This article discusses some of the signs you are in a boring relationship and some of the reasons why the shine often starts to wear off. It also covers steps you can take to fix boredom in a relationship and know if it is time to move on.

CHAPTER TWO

Ways to Deal With Boring People

We've all known people who are charismatic: They seem to light up the room when they walk in. And, when you interact with them, you come away feeling good and energized. On the flip side are people who are bores: They suck the life out of the room, their conversation is tedious, and you can't wait to get away from them.

because "boring people" is a topic that is a source of trouble for me. I define boring people as "people who talk too much."

My favorite people are bright, creative, funny, kind people who conduct reciprocal conversations: that is, they say one thing then stop, and let their friend respond. They listen. The conversation is like a ball of catch: back and forth.

I don't want to be mean, and shut down or walk away from people who gab and gab, but I also don't want to miss out on talking to more fair conversationalists. I have said, "Oh hi. I just now sat down to talk to Janet. Maybe we can talk later." This was true. I felt like that was a good response because it was also fair to Janet.

My boss talks on and on, and is not the least bit interested in what I have to say. I decided that that is okay. This prevents me from oversharing, so her lack of interest in my life is protective. I listen to her instructions for my job, and focus on that part of the conversation.

I have been in seminars where people in love with the sound of their own voice will go on and on, forcing out from the discussion the more timid, and much more interesting, people. I tried such steps as piping up and saying: "I'd like to hear what Jumilla has to say." But, as you can imagine, if Jumilla has been lulled into a coma by the windbag (person over-talking), she won't be ready to speak up when suddenly called out.

Try to become the moderator for discussion groups that you are in. Make a few rules at the beginning: "To make this discussion dynamic, we're going to give everyone a chance to say something, before a person who has already talked can speak again. Each person has 15 seconds (for initial, warm-up type comments) to give their answer. We'll use a talking stick. When it's your turn, you will hold it. While you're holding it, no one else can talk. No comments or responses from others. When you're done, pass on the stick to the next person."

With an individual, allow yourself the privilege of gently interrupting to simply allow yourself the chance to participate in the conversation. If you listen too well, you'll be in the role of a therapist or a one-person audience for a monologue.

CHAPTER THREE

Teaching Kids to Mind Their Manners

Why Manners Count

Back in the late '60s, my father owned a charm school where youngsters in the greater Boston area could transform themselves into gracious adults. In the Fox household, using your fork like a shovel -- or sampling every chocolate in the box -- was a cardinal sin. So when my 19-month-old daughter, Sasha, scribbled on a restaurant wall using a french fry and ketchup as a modified quill and ink, the family legacy was called into question.

I quickly realized that children may be born with a number of innate abilities, but behaving politely is not one of them. And so the onus is on you to teach your little fair lady or gent how to behave in polite society. Read on to learn how to raise a courteous, friendly child who is at home in any social situation.

P's & Q's for Parents

Etiquette guru Emily Post once said, "Manners are a sensitive awareness of the feelings of others. If you have that awareness, you have good manners, no matter what fork you use."

The operative word here is awareness. Around the 18-month mark, a child begins to understand that other people have feelings just like his, so this is the time to start teaching kids that their behavior affects others. Easier said than done, of course. What parent hasn't looked the other way when she hears the greasy thud of a chicken nugget hitting the kitchen wall? Here's what you need to know and how to get started.

Fact #1: Good manners are a good habit. "Behaving politely is a way of life, not just something you pull out when you're at a wedding or fancy restaurant," says Robin Thompson, founder of etiquette-network.com and the Robin Thompson Charm School in Pekin, Illinois. "It's important to start as early as you can so manners become something a child does automatically, whether she is at home or away."

Fact #2: Polite behavior will help your child's social development. Kids who aren't taught social graces from an early age are at a distinct disadvantage, say experts. An ill-mannered child is a turn-off to adults and kids alike; while children aren't likely to be offended by a playmate who neglects to say "excuse me," they don't relish the company of a child who doesn't know how to share or take turns. "You wouldn't send a child off to preschool without a healthy snack," says Sheryl Eberly, mother of three and author of 365 Manners Kids Should Know (Three Rivers Press, 2001). "Sending her into the world without knowing social graces is equally problematic."

Fact #3: Learning manners is a lifelong education. "It won't happen overnight, and you need to take it slowly," says Eberly. Introducing one new social skill a month -- teaching your 2-year-old to say "hello" when another person addresses him, for example, and rewarding him with praise when he does so -- makes the process manageable for everyone.

Equally important is keeping your expectations in check. "There's only so much a small child can do," reminds Eberly. That same 2-year-old is not going to curtsy when ancient Aunt Mabel comes over for Sunday dinner. But she can greet her at the door and sit happily at the table for a limited period of time.

Fact #4: Your behavior counts. "That means that when you ask your partner to pass the salt, you do it with a 'please' and a 'thank you,'" says Eberly. But it goes beyond that. Think about it this way: How would you feel if your child gave a fellow tricycler the finger when he cut her off on the sidewalk? If the thought doesn't thrill you, keep your hands and fingers on the wheel while driving. Inappropriate expressions of anger are rude, too.

Fact #5: Consistency is important. Acquiring good manners takes lots of practice and reinforcement, so make sure that you, your partner, and your caregiver are encouraging (and discouraging) the same behaviors. If your husband lets your kid fling food during meals and you don't, your child won't know what's expected of him.

What to Teach

4 Basic Manners

Basic Table Manners

What to expect: By age 3, your child will be able to eat with a spoon and fork, stay seated at the table for 15 to 20 minutes, and wipe his mouth with a napkin.

What to do: During toddlerhood, offer your child his food on a small, no-break plate; encourage him to use his utensils; discourage him from throwing food by telling him, "We don't throw food on the floor. If you don't want any more, please say 'no thank you.'"

Please and Thank You

What to expect: An 18-month-old may be able to say the words but not necessarily grasp their true meaning. By 2 1/2, kids can link the word to the concept.

What to do: If your child hasn't gotten into the habit, gently prompt him by saying, "What do we say after we get a gift?" or "What do we say when someone gives us a treat?"

Sharing

What to expect: At around 2, a child begins to understand the concept of sharing and turn-taking -- though he won't necessarily relish doing either!

What to do: Encourage your toddler to share with his friends on play dates by giving him two similar toys and helping him offer one to his friend.

Apologizing

What to expect: Though a toddler of about 18 months has a basic understanding of empathy, he can't really understand why he's expected to apologize. By 2 1/2 to 3, he'll understand the concept but may be too caught up in his own affairs to do it on his own.

What to do: When your child snatches a toy from a playmate, discourage the behavior and play on his empathy: "We don't hit; hitting hurts." Then, prompt him to apologize: "When we hurt someone, we say, 'I'm sorry.'"

Let's Talk

Here are Sheryl Eberly's tips on teaching the basic rules of polite conversation.

Look at the party to whom you are speaking or who is speaking to you.Tip: Tell your child to look for what color the person's eyes are.

Answer if you are asked a question.Tip: Gently prompt your child to speak. Let him know that it's okay to say "I don't know."

Don't speak until the person you are speaking with is finished.Tip: Encourage patience by telling your child to count to five before speaking.

Don't interrupt unless it's an emergency; if a friend is sick, for instance, or someone needs to use the bathroom. If you must interrupt, say "Excuse me."Tip: Develop a signal your child can use to indicate that he needs you -- raising his index finger, for example.

Play-Date Protocol

Play dates are a great opportunity to practice manners. Here's how to ensure your child is on his best behavior.

Set your child up for success. Young children behave well when they're rested and comfortable. Plan play dates around naps and meals.

Gently remind him of your expectations. Before you go, tell your child that he has to share and say "please" and "thank you."

Prompt him when he forgets to be mannerly. If your child takes a snack from your host without comment, for example, say, "Please thank Mrs. Jones for the cookie."

Step in when things get hairy. During the play date, someone will inevitably hit, bite, or toy-snatch. If your child is the instigator, say, "That made your friend feel bad. Let's make him feel better by saying that we're sorry."

Help him thank his host. When you leave, remind your child he had fun and prompt him to say "thank you."

Mr., Mrs., or Ms.?

Should your child call your best friend Jane or Mrs. Jones? Ultimately, say manners experts, it's up to your friend. However, some grown-ups prefer more formality than others, so err on the side of politeness. Introduce adults as "Mr." or "Mrs." and let the adult in question say, "Please call me Al," if that's his preference.

Gross Behavior

Q. Help! My 2-11/2-year-old is a pathological nose-picker. To top it off, she's learning to use the potty, so she's constantly talking about pee and poop. All told, she presents a pretty gross package. Is there anything I can do?

The nose-picking is definitely the easiest thing to deal with. "When you see her going for her nose, just offer her a tissue," says Thompson. "Don't make a big deal out of it." Toddlers are trying to figure out exactly what they can get away with and what they can't. Showing displeasure may make your daughter want to engage in the behavior even more.

As for the potty talk, you're going to have to deal with it for a while. Saying the words is a way for your child to connect the urge with the act -- and that's a good thing. When she uses the words for shock value, treat the situation the same way you would the nose-picking: In a matter-of-fact manner, ask her if she needs to use the potty. If the answer is no, carry on with what you were doing. Chances are, she won't be as tempted to use these words if she can't get a rise out of you.

5 Discipline Strategies to Teach Kids Classic Manners

A well-mannered child will stand out in today's world for all the right reasons. Saying, "Please" and "thank you," and using good table manners will get your child noticed by teachers and other parents.

Teaching good manners can seem a little tricky, however. It can be hard to convince a child to follow basic manners when his peers at school might not be doing so.

Help your child master basic manners with these discipline strategies:

1. Praise Your Child's Use of Manners

Praise your child whenever you catch him using good manners. For young children, this may mean saying, "Great job remembering to say 'thank you.'"

Praise older kids for putting their phone away when they're at the dinner table or for shaking hands when greeting a new person.

If you've got a younger child, provide praise right away. Say, "You did a nice job thanking Grandma for that gift."

Don't embarrass a teen by praising him in front of other people. Instead, have a private conversation about how you appreciate that he behaved politely toward guests at a family gathering or give him positive feedback on how he handled an interaction with a store clerk.

2. Model Polite Behavior

The best way to teach your child any new skill is to be a good role model. When your child sees you speaking politely to others and using your manners, he'll pick up on that.

Pay attention to how you interact with your spouse or close family members. Sometimes, it's easy to forget to use manners with the people you feel most comfortable with.

Send thank you notes, ask for things politely, and show appreciation when people are kind. Whether you're in line at the grocery store or you're calling your doctor's office, your kids are paying attention to your behavior.

And be careful about how you handle situations when you're upset. If you're angry with someone, do you tend to raise your voice? Do you use harsh words when you think someone has treated you unfairly? Your message about the importance of using manners won't be heard if you don't model how to behave politely and respectfully.

10 Specific Manners Your Kids Need to Know

If we've heard it once, we've heard it a thousand times. It goes like this: Today's young people just don't have any manners. When I was young, children were more mannerly. A little respect could go a long way. Good manners for kids are not automatic nor do they develop without some deliberate teaching and modeling by the adults. It's our responsibility to "train children in the way they should go," as the proverb suggests.

Here's the payoff: Once learned, good manners make everyone's life more pleasant. For an added bonus: If your kids have well-practiced manners, they're going to get hired first when it's time to go to work, and they'll likely be more successful on the job. Societies that function on a high level are called civilizations for a reason; civility is a prerequisite. Likewise, families that learn to practice good manners don't only function smoothly on the outside, they experience more positives and reduced conflict internally. It's a direct result of practiced civility.

So let's talk about 10 good manners for kids to know:

1. Put others first.

This could be the only point we need to make because it's at the root of all the others. This principle is manifest in holding doors, stepping aside, offering the last cookie, giving up your seat, changing a tire, carrying groceries, and offering a hand.

2. Polite phone protocol.

This item could have its own list. Turn the phone off during meals, movies, classes, and conversations. This includes texting. Bottom line: Give 100% attention to the people you are physically with. Your phone has a voice mail feature, use it.

3. Thank you note.

There are two kinds of people in this world: those who write thank you notes for gifts or special occasions and those who don't. Teach your kids to write thank you notes and they will have understood a fundamental concept. Nothing elaborate is necessary, but the effect is always memorable.

4. Open the door for others.

Contrary to popular myth, this is not a chauvinistic practice. Doorholders open for their peers, their mothers, their dads, and strangers. They also yield the sidewalk and hold the elevator. There's no stopping them. Good manners always say, "After you."

5. Use thank you and you're welcome routinely in conversation.

Simple but powerful. Help the kids make it a habit. This is one you need to model at your end.

6. Shake hands and make eye contact.

Teach kids to shake hands, to make eye contact, and to offer a word of welcome when they meet new people or when others visit the home. It may be a cliché to say first impressions make a big impact, but it's a cliché because it's true.

7. Teach them to offer to serve people who enter your home.

Make it routine. May I take your coat? Would you like a glass of water? Let me take your bags. People who visit are our guests. This is a key lesson, no matter what a child's age.

8. Stand up when an elder enters the room.

Many adults have forgotten this gem. It's a sign of respect no matter what our age. Grandparents. Aunts and uncles. Teachers. Any visitor to the home. Teach children to stand as a sign of respect.

9. Be polite to people who serve.

This means make eye contact and turn your phone off when talking to the cashier at the fast food restaurant or at the grocery store. It means being respectful to the server at the restaurant. It means saying thank you when you're given food or change. Try thanking the bus driver for the ride home or a soldier for serving our country.

10. Practice manners at family mealtimes.

Family dinners can be a perfect venue for manners. Demonstrate, practice, model, question, prompt. No TV, no phones, and no distractions from polite interaction. Please pass the potatoes. Thanks. Can I get that for you? Mom, can I pour you a glass of water? The family unit is the most important venue to learn social graces and family mealtimes are maybe our best opportunity.

3. Role-Play Tricky Situations

Role-playing gives kids an opportunity to practice their skills. It can be a helpful strategy when you're entering into a new situation or when you're facing some complicated circumstances.

If your 5-year-old has invited friends to his birthday party, role-play how to use manners while opening presents. Help him practice how to thank people for his gift and how to respond if he opens a gift that he doesn't particularly like.

Sit down with your child and say, "What would you do if..." and then see what he has to say. Pretend to be a friend or another adult and see how your child responds to specific situations. Then, provide feedback and help your child discover how to behave politely and respectfully in various scenarios.

4. Provide a Brief Explanation

Avoid lecturing or telling long-winded tales. Instead, simply state the reason why a specific behavior may not be appreciated.

Kids are more likely to remember their manners and specific etiquette rules when you provide a brief explanation about why a particular behavior is considered impolite or rude.

If your child is chewing with his mouth open, say, "People don't want to see the food in your mouth when they're trying to eat." If you make a big deal about it, you may inadvertently encourage the behavior to continue.

But, if you can just state the reason in a calm and matter-of-fact manner, it can serve as a reminder for your child about why other people may not appreciate what he's doing.

5. Keep Your Expectations Age-Appropriate

Make sure that your expectations are appropriate to your child's age and developmental level. You can start working with a toddler on the basics of saying "please," "thank you," and "sorry."

By the time your child's a teenager, you should be focusing on advanced skills like phone etiquette and more complex communication skills.

Sometimes it's helpful to really focus on one area at a time—like basic table manners—before moving onto other skills. If you give your child too much to learn at once he may become overwhelmed. It's common too for previous skills to be revisited from time to time to make sure your child is remembering to use them.

100 Ways to Praise Your Child

Learning new skills can be difficult at times, but you'd be surprised how far a little encouragement can go. Try some of these to start, or add your own below!

That's Incredible!
How Extraordinary!
You're Very Talented!
Outstanding Performance!
Far Out!
Great!
Very Brave!
Marvelous!
I Can't Get Over It!
Wonderful!
You Figured It Out!
You Should Be Proud!
Amazing Effort!
Unbelievable Work!
You're the Greatest!
Phenomenal!
You've Got It!
Superb!
How Original!
You're Special!
Cool!
Excellent!
Congratulations!
Your Project is First Rate!
Way To Go!
You've Outdone Yourself!
You're Super!
Thumbs Up!
What A Great Listener!
Your Help Counts!
You Make Me Smile!
You Came Through!
Terrific!
You Tried Hard!
You're A Pleasure To Know!

Fabulous!
Your Effort Really Shows!
You Made It Happen!
What A Genius Idea!
You're A Real Trooper!
It Couldn't Be Better!
Bravo!
You're A Champ!
You're Unique!
Exceptional!
You Set A Good Example!
Right On!
Fantastic Work!
Breathtaking!
Keep Up The Good Work!
Clever!
Awesome!
I Knew You Had It In You!
You've Made Progress!
Magnificent!
Your Work Is Out of Sight!
What An Imagination!
It's Everything I Hoped For!
Brilliant!
Stupendous!
You're Sensational!
Very Good!
You're A-OK!
You Made The Difference!
Good For You!
A+ Work!
You're So Kind!
Take A Bow!
Super Job!
How Thoughtful of You!
You're Sharp!
Nice Going!
Class Act!

Well Done!
Thanks For Helping!
You're Inspiring!
How Artistic!
You Go The Extra Mile!
You've Earned My Respect!
Hooray For You!
You're A Joy!
You're A Shining Star!
You're #1!
You're Amazing!
What A Great Idea!
Great Answer!
Great Discovery!
Extra Special Work!
You Deserve A Hug
You're Getting Better!
Wow!
You're Tops!
You're Catching On!
You're Neat!
You're Very Responsible!
You've Got What It Takes!
Spectacular Work!
You're A Winner!
Thanks For Caring!
Beautiful!

9 Great Ways to Be Exceptionally Boring

Can you choose whether you are an interesting person or a dull person? To a large extent you can. There are things you can do to make your company and your conversation interesting and there are things you can do that will make you boring. If you want to be dull try the following list. If you want to be interesting do the opposite:

Talk a lot about yourself. Tell people about your and your life. Don't ask questions. Don't show an interest in other people and above all do not listen to what they say.

Watch a lot of TV. Do not waste time reading, going out or with hobbies – just keep up with soaps, sport and popular entertainment programs.

Do the same things. Get into a regular routine and do not diverge from it. Don't try anything new or adventurous.

Don't waste time on books or the arts. Avoid the cinema, the theatre, literature, magazines, new kinds of music or live performances.

Stay at home. Don't waste time and money travelling to new places and experiencing different cultures, activities or lifestyles.

Stick with the same group of friends. Keep to the people you have known for a long time. Do not go out of your way to meet people or make new friends.

Do not have goals or a plan. Drift along the way you are doing now. Do not set yourself difficult objectives that you might not achieve. Go with the flow and see what happens.

Never change your mind. Once you have a simple and clear view of the world, stick with it. Do not let new facts or opinions sway you. Stay firmly committed to what you know and brush aside uncomfortable ideas.

Take very poor care of yourself. Drink a lot of alcohol, eat a lot of fatty foods, and get very little exercise.

What Makes You Seem Like One Of The Boring Men To A Woman?

If you're single, you know how hard it is to meet someone who you can hit it off instantly. The chances of that happening can dwindle quickly if you come across as one of those boring men who can put their date to sleep. Women are more easily bored than you think. Don't mistake that approving smile as an expression of her interest, she might just be trying to be nice.

If you are a boring date, she's probably already texting her friend to call her with an emergency, or making a mental note of all the laundry she needs to do. With that, goes the possibility of a second date.

To break free from this vicious circle of first dates that lead nowhere, we suggest you introspect to see if you fit in the category of boring guys. But since nobody really likes to deem themselves boring, you've probably never thought about acknowledging it. To help you with that, we're decoding what makes a man boring to a woman.

It is no secret that men and women are wired differently. What seems interesting and engaging to you may bore the living daylights out of her.

So, it is only sensible to view what constitutes boring men from a woman's perspective. For example, that sporting event you saw last night might be all the rage amongst your guy friends, but unless she's a huge fan herself, she probably doesn't care about who scored the winning goal or shot, and so she definitely won't be needing the second-by-second replay.

Even if you're not talking about things like sports and wrestling on dates, you still might come across as boring without even realizing it. Think about it, would you want your date to talk about something that you're not one bit interested in? Let's figure out how not to be boring after we take a look at the signs of boring men, so you can identify the problem at least. Here is our lowdown on the signs of a boring guy:

1. Boring men are steeped in patriarchal privilege

One boring personality trait in men is their allegiance to the age old norms of patriarchy. Women are bored with men that seem to be cast out of the same mold. The one who aspires to be the "man of the house" and is unaware of his privilege. The man who likes to order for his date at restaurants and doesn't believe in going Dutch or women picking up the tab.

The man who says things like "I can allow my life partner to work" as if it's a decision he believes he gets to make. Who comments on the length of a woman's dress or the number of drinks she's had. All boring, boring, very boring. Break the mold! Talk to women without offending them, and we might be interested in a conversation.

2. They brag to no end

Bragging does not just put you in the category of boring guys but also makes you annoying. Would you care if we told you about the debate competition we won in high school or the remarks we got on a recent appraisal at work? No? Yeah, we neither.

This is not to say that we don't respect your achievements. But it's just not polite date conversation. We are not here for a TedTalk, are we? These things can be discussed once two people grow closer and genuinely want to know about the smallest details of each other's lives.

By bringing this up during initial dates, you're condemning yourself to the zone of boring men, or the ones who think they're the best thing that ever happened to planet Earth. Snap out of this bad dating habit NOW.

3. Complete lack of courtesy

No, we do not mean chivalry. We don't want you to open doors and hold out chairs for us. Or even pick up the bill every single time. We're talking basic courtesies like not yelling at the waiter or picking a fight in a bar when we are with you. For the love of God, make eye contact when you talk to a woman, don't just stare at her breasts. Instant turn off, instant rejection.

Basic courtesies are expected from anyone, be it a date or a coworker. If you show up thirty minutes late to a date, forget about trying to figure out "how to not be boring with a girl", first think about the sincere apology that you so owe her, otherwise there won't be a girl for you to entertain.

4. Cheesy one-liners will make us see you as boring men

Yes, we do not want you to take our hand, look us in the eye and recite cringy couplets. The same goes for those cheesy one-liners as well. Life isn't a Hollywood movie. Let's keep it as real as it can get. All this mush is so done to death that it instantly makes us zone out.

Especially when it's one of those one-liners we've all heard and seen before. "Did it hurt?" I don't know if it hurt for me, but it's sure going to hurt your ego when I don't even let you get to the end of this incredibly over-used "pick-up line". The minute you use a recycled one-liner on someone, expect to be hit with something along the lines of "Men are boring, please leave me alone."

5. Mansplaining counts as boring personality traits

Your condescending responses to what we have to say or breaking down nuggets of information like we're 5-year-olds, counts as one of those boring personality traits that make us want to bolt. We can talk about car engines and investments and politics. Don't act surprised, let go of your stereotypical misconceptions, and don't make the mistake of brushing off our opinions as invalid just because they're coming from a woman.

When a man thinks he knows more about something than a woman even though she may be an expert in the field, solely because he's a man, it's always an instant turn-off.

6. An urgency to get into our pants

If you're too eager to get into her pants, it won't go down well

Unfortunately, every woman has been through this. The initial conversations go well, we're hitting it off until boom, the guy creepily slides in the most sexual remark you've ever heard. It's not just boring, it's absurd. You barely know her, what do you expect her to say to, "What would you like me to do to you in bed"? Nothing. Leave me alone.

We'll get there, when and if we get there. If you're going to sit around and make us feel like the sole reason why you're out with us is to get into our pants, you're going to make one helluva boring date. No self-respecting woman is going to give you a second chance. Hold off the sexual overtures and innuendos until it's appropriate.

7. Boring men are not well-read

It's perfectly all right if we don't have the same taste in books or if you have not heard of that one book we consider a cult classic. But if you just don't read at all or don't have an interesting personality, you will invariably turn out to be one of those boring men who doesn't know how to strike an interesting conversation.

Imagine she starts talking about her favorite movie, and you say you aren't into movies. She proceeds to talk about her favorite pop band, and you don't listen to pop music. Give her something to work with, put forth the best aspects of your personality. No woman is looking to be dating a boring guy.

8. A constricted worldview makes you boring

We know we're dating a boring guy when your worldview is closed, outdated, and constricted. It's a clear sign that you've made no effort to keep up with the times, absorb different perspectives on situations and form a unique opinion on things.

From climate change to geo-politics and everything else in between, if your ideas seem borrowed and stale, we're not going to be interested. A lack of will to change becomes an absolute deal-breaker.

9. Lacking a sense of humour

Wit is a sign of intelligence, and it attracts a woman a whole lot more than your fat paycheck or swanky car. If you completely lack a sense of humor and just cannot make us laugh, you're not going to be able to hold our interest for long. We may make it through one boring date with you, or two, but it is not going to go far.

If you're stressing out too much about this one, don't let it get to your head. Making a girl laugh isn't as hard as it seems, sometimes all it takes is having a genuine conversation with her without urgently trying to impress or flirt.

10. Boring men lack a sense of adventure

By adventure, we don't mean that to be interesting you have to jump off planes and cliffs, obviously, but having an adventurous streak that eggs you on to soak up new experiences in life. What's more boring than spending your entire life doing the same things, day after day, year after year?

If you can't mix things up a little, you're displaying one of the classic signs of a boring guy. Try out that adventure sport you've always been afraid to try, travel to the places you've always wanted to go to. Make a few memories, so you don't come across as the blandest person alive.

So, take a long, hard look at these signs of a boring guy, and see where you can make amends to improve your prospects of dating successfully. If you've figured out you could use some work on conversation skills, here are a bunch of tips on how to not be boring with a girl that should help you out.

How To Not Be Boring When Talking To Women

If you've never really been the funniest of the bunch or aren't even too big on traveling and collecting the most enthralling stories, don't worry too much. Figuring out how to not be boring is as easy as being comfortable in your own skin, and confidently putting your best foot forward. The following tips should help:

1. You don't have to constantly try to impress her

A conversation isn't a laugh-a-thon where you have to make her laugh every two minutes. When the pressure wears off, you'll feel a lot more at ease in your conversation. We'd recommend not overdoing it with the puns about her name, or better yet, avoid them altogether. Puns can very quickly go from receiving an "aww!" to an "okay, stop."

2. Ask about her

Talking to someone isn't a one-way street, it requires equal effort from both ends. Try to notice if she's interested in you, ask her questions about herself, make her feel like you genuinely want to know her. Is she a beer person or a teetotaler? Does she enjoy beaches or the mountains? A simple way to avoid being hit with the "men are boring" tag is to just be genuinely interested in your date.

3. Talk about mutual interests

If you're talking about Albert Camus and his thoughts on existentialism, it might not be the most gripping conversation (unless she's a philosophy nerd herself). Interesting ways to chat and make the conversation flow only take place if you talk about the things she's interested in. Try not to talk about that niche thing you and only 18 other people on the specific subreddit are interested in. You have to talk about things you know she likes too.

Though you might be stressing about it, how to not be boring with a girl is really as simple as that. Be yourself, be courteous and have conversations about things you know she's interested in. Boring men tend to think they're the belle of the ball (Dunning-Kruger, much?), so if you know of someone who's boring, send them this article. It might just do them some good.

1. What are the signs of a boring relationship?

A boring relationship is one in which neither partner feels too excited to meet each other and don't do too many things together. In such a relationship, partners might not even have too many things in common or anything to talk about.

2. What to do if you think you are boring?

If you think you are boring, try to develop some new hobbies to enrich your personality. Make new friends, have a few new experiences, and make memories. The more you find yourself, the more interesting you'll become.

3. What makes a boyfriend boring?

A boyfriend who doesn't like to talk too much or doesn't like to get out of the house at all can be considered a boring boyfriend. Though their likes may differ from their partner, someone who's unwilling to do anything fun at all might be justifiably termed as boring.

How to Be a Less Boring Person

Some people may want to break out of their shell and become more exciting to themselves and to others. People who are not boring are often outgoing and adventurous. In order to be a less boring person, it's important to be open to others, have a sense of humor, and be adventurous. Being a less boring person can change your personal interactions, your social world, and your daily life.

Finding Adventures to Make You Less Boring

1

Show interest in a wide variety of people, places, and things. If you try to get out of your comfort zone of knowledge, you will learn more interesting things. Boring people are often not interested in people other than themselves, which makes them less fun to be around.

Visit new neighborhoods and restaurants. Don't just go to the same place everyday, since you'll never experience anything new.

Read about different people that are not like you. This can be people from a different country, region, ethnic group, or gender.

Listen to different genres of music. Even if you don't always understand it at first, try listening to new and interesting music that comes from different backgrounds than your own.

Try learning a new skill or taking up a new hobby. Learning a new skill or hobby can force you to challenge yourself. A new hobby or skill can be a fun thing to talk to people about and can show that you are an interesting person rather than something who doesn't enjoy learning new things.[1]

Hobbies can also introduce you to new people who share your hobby. Learning how to play guitar with others can make you new friends.

Taking up a hobby like cooking can also give you something that you can do and talk about with others. If your hobby is relatable, people will be interested to learn more about it.

Travel to new and exciting locations. Traveling broadens your perspective on life and gives you interesting stories to tell others. Even if you're just going to the next state over, traveling somewhere always gives you interesting stories to tell rather than boring stories from the sames places you always go.

Look for cheap flights from your airport. There may be some travel deals to exotic or local places.

Experience new cultures. Taking part in different cultures can broad your horizons.

Join interesting clubs or groups. Getting involved in activities outside of work or school can give you fun things to talk about. It also shows that you are interested in expanding your horizons and not just hanging around the same people doing the same things.

Find an intramural sports league. Even if you're only playing sports as a hobby, it can have great social benefits and personal fulfillment for you.

Look for volunteer groups that you might find interesting. There are many volunteer groups that might match your interests. Helping other people can make you feel better as well.

Get creative in your experiences. Something exciting like skydiving lets others now you're up for a challenge. It also shows you like to try new things and want to have fun while doing different things.

Try skydiving by yourself or with a group. It can be a fun activity that is a once in a life time experience.

Take up new challenges like rock climbing. Outdoor activities like hiking can also be a fun way to have creative experiences and become a less boring person.

Listen to others when they're talking. If you're talking to other people, this means you are also listening to what they have to say. Boring people don't listen, but instead only wait for the other person to stop talking so they can start; instead, always listen to others so you can have a two-way conversation with them.

Pay attention to the other person's body language. If they are slouched, have their arms crossed, or seem disengaged, they may be bored by your conversation.

Ask plenty of questions about the other person. Try to avoid standard conversation starters like "What do you do for a living?" but instead ask fun questions like "What's the best part of your week?" or "What makes you feel passionate?

Share your opinions. Boring people often have no opinions or are afraid to share their opinions. Sharing your opinions shows that are paying attention and have something to contribute.

If you disagree with someone, be considerate of their opinion. Don't attack them, but show that you are listening and engaging with them.

When you do share your opinion, make sure to know both sides of the conversation. Otherwise, you may come across as uninformed.

Have fun when you're talking to others. Look for opportunities to have a good time. Boring people are often inhibited or afraid to do something that seems crazy; instead, try to always look for a way to have fun with others.

If you have any skills or talents, show them off. Don't make yourself the center of attention, but find ways to show that you know how to do things.

Try not to worry too much what others think. If you're feeling and acting natural, that will make you a less boring person.

Be positive about your life. Boring people often moan about their life and work, whereas less boring people see life more positively. Talk about the things you care about, not the things that bother you.

If you are talking to people about what you are excited about in life, you are more interesting and engaging to others. Being passionate really shows through in your nonverbal body language.

Let other people shine. Focus on the talents and skills of other people as well. When you're talking to them, ask them about things they care about, so you don't make the conversation all about you.

Don't be conceited. Try not to worry about how you come off to others. If other people are the center of attention, that does not make you a boring person.

Smile when you're talking to others. A grin shows that you approach life with a positive attitude and that you're interested in making friends. If you have a blank or sad expression on your face, you'll come across as boring and disengaged to others.

Smiling makes you feel happier and more open to new situations. It can really improve your mood and make you more likely to talk to others.

When you smile at others, it's often contagious. They'll want to smile back at you and feel more receptive when talking to you.

Make laughter a priority. If laughter is important to you, then you will make an effort to laugh when you're around others. It is part of your personality to be a person full of laughter, which shows you feel joy in life. In contrast, boring people often seem joyless and do not laugh often.[13]

Laughter brings people closer together. It bonds them together socially through the shared experience of laughter.

If you make laughter a priority, this shows that are a joyful person. It shows that you are in touch with yourself and others.

Don't be scared to be wacky or zany. Sometimes, it's good to dance like a goofball, have unusual conversations, or do silly things. Holding back your silly side from others may close you off from them and make them think of you as a boring person.

Always involve others in silliness. Don't be a clown for others, but instead bring them into any fun activity you are doing.

Being silly also shows that you don't care too much about what others are thinking. You are interested and engaged in others, but not reliant on them for your sense of self-worth.

Don't wait for others to begin having fun. Boring people often wait for others to entertain them. Instead, start the fun by yourself and encourage others to join in engaging in fun and playful activities.

Start joking with others when the opportunity arises. They may be willing to join in the fun, but were just waiting for others to start.

Do something silly or outrageous to gauge everyone's reaction. If they are amused or entertained, then you know that they are also interested in laughing and having a good time.

Try to look at things from a unique perspective. Humor is a sign of intelligence and flexibility in terms of outlook. Boring people often seem inflexible and not willing to change their perspective.

When people are talking, think of funny ways to take their words or their actions. Don't insult them, but try to find the humor in any conversation.

Don't be afraid to make fun of yourself. Making fun of yourself shows that you do not take yourself too seriously.

CHAPTER FOUR

100 Fun Things to Do When Bored To Help You Stay Sane

With smartphones and Netflix constantly at our fingertips, being bored and stuck feeling like there's nothing to do almost doesn't seem possible... almost. But now, with what seems to be the never-ending social distancing, boredom has become completely and utterly inevitable.

So, when it feels like the seconds are just dragging on, here are 100 fun things to do when you're bored! From completing a jigsaw puzzle or conducting your own wine tasting to making an Insta account for your pet or starting a blog, you'll have no excuse to say "I'm bored!" ever again.

100 Things to Do When Bored

1. Tye dye T-shirts.

Tye dye white T-shirts in a matching color scheme with your kids. When the shirts are dried, have an inside photoshoot and post the photos to Instagram.

4. Make your own movie.

Using your smartphone, shoot a movie or re-create one using household props. Use editing software like iMovie to put it all together.

5. Create slime with your kids.

Keep your kids entertained for hours with just glue, eye contact solution, and food coloring. Look up the recipes for other slime variations to keep the fun going.

6. Read a book.

Dust off your favorite book and read it from cover-to-cover. If the book made it to the silver screen, watch the movie adaptation and make notes to compare!

7. Go on a walk.

The CDC says that walking outside is still allowed (and encouraged)! Just be mindful to keep a 6-foot distance between yourself and others.

8. Bake something sweet.

Nothing is more delicious than a fresh cookie out of the oven. Bake up a storm using classic recipes found online or be daring and create your own.

9. Complete a jigsaw puzzle.

Set up a little puzzle station in your living room and work on it between Netflix binges.

10. Play an instrument.

If it doesn't bother your neighbors, pick up and learn a small instrument like the ukulele.

11. Learn a new language.

With free apps, like Duolingo, now is a great time to learn a foreign language for your next trip.

12. Start journaling.

Keeping a journal or a diary is a great way to navigate through tough feelings while also killing some time.

13. Pick up a new hobby.

Knitting and embroidery are an awesome way to bring a personal touch to your wardrobe and home decor. Check out some YouTube tutorials on what the perfect stitch is for a circle scarf.

14. Play an old game from your childhood.

Whether it's a board game like Clue or a video game like Kingdom Hearts, playing a childhood favorite game will not only kill some time but also bring back some serious childhood nostalgia.

15. Organize your house.

Make like Marie Kondo and spark some joy by reorganizing your closets and de-cluttering your surroundings.

Related: 125 Ways to Keep Kids Entertained

16. Make mixed playlists.

With music-sharing apps like Spotify or Pandora, create your own personalized playlists and share them with friends.

17. Perfect an old family recipe.

Does your family have a recipe that's been passed down for generations? Take this time to learn and perfect it so all your relatives will say it's better than grandma's by Christmas.

18. Learn a tabletop role-playing game.

Back in the day, games like Dungeons and Dragons may have been only for nerds but, it turns out, it's a great way to kill some time. All you need for the game are some dice, friends, and imagination.

19. Create your own signature cocktail.

If someone created a drink after you, what would be in it? Create it and make sure to put it on the menu at your next dinner party.

20. Order some takeout.

While many restaurants are closed for dine-in customers, many are still offering delivery and pickup options. Use apps like Seamless or Uber Eats to support your favorite local grub spot.

21. Have an indoor picnic.

Clear out the living room, set down a blanket, and make your own picnic lunch without having to step outside.

22. Pickle some veggies.

Slice some vegetables like cucumbers and onion and throw them in a mason jar filled with vinegar and seasonings. Seal the jar and let it sit for a while until your next barbecue for some pickled toppings.

23. Get some Christmas shopping done.

If you're still having some stressful holiday-related flashbacks, why not tackle it early this year and make some headway on your 2020 Christmas list.

24. Write a gratitude list.

Remind yourself that there is a light at the end of the tunnel by counting your blessings. Use cute stationery or your favorite pen to make it extra special.

25. Cook an extravagant meal.

Have a date night at home inspired by the likes of Gordon Ramsey and Julia Child. Test your culinary skills by cooking an involved recipe like beef Wellington or coq au vin.

26. Have ice cream for dinner.

Create a little of your own sunshine by making every 5 year old's dream come true: ice cream for dinner! Set up a sundae bar in your kitchen with various toppings and different flavors (don't forget the whipped cream!).

27. Take a bubble bath.

In these tense times, a bubble bath can be a great way to unwind. Add a little aromatherapy with calming scents like lavender or jasmine to increase your zen.

(iStock)

28. Make a smoothie.

In long periods of downtime, it's easy to mindlessly snack on junk food. Create a healthier alternative by mixing together your own frozen fruit concoction.

29. Read a New York Times Best Seller.

Find the New York Times Best Seller list from the year you were born. Choose the number one choice and see if it's still timeless with age.

30. Watch all the "Best Picture" Oscar-winning films from the past decade.

See how these films stand out from the rest. Go through the Oscar's Best Picture winner list, choose what stands out to you, and pop the popcorn.

31. Try some Pinterest hacks.

Go through your favorite Pinterest board and see what hacks you can do around the house. Make note of the ones that work.

32. Conduct your own wine tasting.

Open the bottles you have already in the house. Make up a story about the grapes and how they ended up turning into wine.

33. Work on your financial planning.

With breaking news changing from day-to-day, it may be a good time to go over your annual budget and see what needs to be adjusted.

34. Camp indoors.

Clear out the living room and build a fort or pitch a tent to bring some of the outdoors, inside! If you really want to go all out, roll out some sleeping bags and hang up some glow-in-the-dark stars for some sweet memories.

35. Interview your grandparents.

Give your grandparents a call and ask them all about their lives. Record the conversation using your phone.

36, Master your favorite drink.

Whether it's Manhattan or a glass of old-fashioned lemonade, gather supplies and ingredients and craft it to perfection.

37. Take a virtual visit to the zoo.

Do you have a future wildlife expert living among you? Give the kids a lesson in zoology and see what the animals are up to by checking out the live cameras at the San Diego Zoo!

38. Visit the world with Google Earth.

Even though tickets for flights around the world are at an all-time low, it is strongly advised not to travel further than your own backyard. If adventure is calling your name, load up Google Earth, type in your dream destination, and give yourself a virtual tour.

39. Give yourself a mani/pedi.

Who needs the salon? Bust out your favorite color of polish and paint them to your heart's content. Be sure to look at YouTube tutorials to learn how to do fun designs!

40. Learn a new style of dance.

Use this time to watch YouTube tutorials and learn how to boogie in different ways. Dancing like belly dancing and shuffling are great ways to stay in shape without the gym.

41. Marathon classic film series.

Transform your living room into a movie theater with popcorn and snacks and marathon classic films, like Star Wars or Back to the Future! Bonus points if you can come up with fun ways to watch the series in a different order.

42. Meditate.

Calm your mind by taking 10 minutes or more to meditate and quiet your thoughts. Browse through YouTube for some guided meditations or download apps like Headspace for some quick sessions.

43. Give yourself a makeover.

Face masks, moisturizers, and skincare galore! Treat yourself to a 10 step skincare routine and get your pamper on.

Related: 50+ Ways to Beat Cabin Fever During Coronavirus Social Distancing

44. Feng shui your living room.

Give your furniture more of a role in your calm by researching the philosophy of feng shui and seeing what's best for your home.

45. Buy gift cards online from your favorite neighborhood shops.

With uncertain times, most local businesses are being forced to close without knowing if they can re-open. Support your local neighborhood by buying gift certificates now and then use later.

46. Write a book with your family.

Have each family member create one character. Then have one person start by writing a chapter, then hand to the next person to write chapter two, and so forth. Continue until the story ends!

47. Conduct a Scrabble tournament.

With March Madness canceled, conduct your own Scrabble tournament with your family. Have your kids fill out brackets to predict the winner!

48. Host a virtual meet-up.

If quarantining has left you more distant than social, consider coordinating a video hangout with loved ones. Video sharing software like Zoom or Skype can be used to play online games with each other and extensions like Netflix Party can be used for a virtual movie night!

49. Write a letter.

Be like a heroine in a Jane Austin novel and write a letter by hand. Send it off to a loved one and wait for a response.

50. Sleep.

Even if you're not feeling sick, one of the best ways to give your immune system a boost during this pandemic is loads and loads of rest. Being sleep deprived can weaken your immunity cells and increase your chances of getting sick. Taking a quick nap whenever you're looking to pass the time can give your immune system a fighting chance.

51. Plant a garden.

What better time to start growing your own produce than now when you're home so much? If you don't have a backyard, don't worry; you can try planting a small herb garden you can keep inside.

52. Teach your pet some new tricks.

Take advantage of the fact that you have a pet in your life and spend some extra time teaching it some fun tricks. You can even get your kids involved and show off what you taught your pet via FaceTime to your friends and family.

53. Memorize where all the states are on the map.

You'd be surprised that a lot of Americans can't name all 50 states, let alone point out where each of them is on the map. Challenge yourself to beat those odds by memorizing every state's name and its location.

54. Learn how to make earrings on YouTube.

You might not be going into as many stores lately, so why not learn how to make some new accessories yourself? With YouTube tutorials, you can find out what items you need to purchase and how you can create your dream jewelry at home for a fraction of the cost!

55. Hang up some twinkle lights.

Since you're spending more time than ever at home, think about making your outdoor space more magical by adding some twinkle lights to it. You can hang them on your fence, from your trees or overhead on your deck.

56. Complete a crossword.

Challenge yourself to a mind game, like a crossword. You can find one in a newspaper, magazine or even online that you can print out.

57.Landscape your yard.

No matter if you add flowers, bushes, re-mulch or even add a water fountain to your yard, landscaping is something that'll keep you from being bored. You can do a little or as much as you'd like each day. To get started, check out Pinterest for some inspiration.

58. Color-code your bookshelf.

Your bookshelf will look like it's straight out of a magazine once you color-code it. You can arrange them from lightest to darkest colors, warm colors to cool colors or in the order of a rainbow (red, orange, yellow, green, blue, indigo, violet.)

59. Sign up for a paint and sip class.

Whether you decide to attend with a friend or by yourself, you'll have a ball participating in an online paint and sip class. Once you're done, you'll have a new piece of art to decorate your home with.

60. Take an online barre class.

Find a barre class on YouTube that you can follow from home, or join a virtual one that is offered online. It'll help you feel a bit more normalcy with everything going on if you can add it to your routine a few times a week.

61. Take a virtual museum tour.

You'll be surprised to know that several popular museums are offering virtual tours you can attend! So even if you don't live near a museum that's in NYC or Paris, you can "go to it" from your home.

62. Donate your clothes.

Chances are your closet is filled with tons of things you no longer wear, right? Take some time to go through your belongings and filter out things you haven't worn in a long time and things that no longer fit you. Then, donate those tops, pants and shoes to a shelter or a place like Plato's Closet, Buffalo Exchange or Salvation Army.

63. Clean out your pantry.

Don't just organize your pantry, de-clutter it! Tossing out junk foods and items that you want to try to wean out of your diet will help you be less tempted to eat poorly while you're at home.

64. Make a virtual TikTok recipe.

Not all TikToks are dance-related—there are tons of cool and easy recipes on there, too. Find one that appeals to you and give it a shot! Your kids will love that you were inspired by the app.

65. Start a blog.

Even if you've never thought about blogging before, now's the perfect time for that. You can make it about something you enjoy, like fashion, or even about your life during quarantine.

67. Set up an Instagram for your pet.

If you have a pet, then there's no doubt that your phone is filled with tons of adorable pics and videos of them. Have some fun showing them off by setting up an Instagram page just for them. It'll be a great way to connect with other animal lovers and create a scrapbook for your fur baby.

68. Update your resume.

If you're really bored, pull up your resume on your computer one afternoon. Then, take time to re-word it and re-organize it.

69. Reach out to someone you haven't seen in a while.

Feeling lonely and disconnected from people because of Covid restrictions is normal, so even if you haven't spoken to a friend or family member in a long time, try rekindling that relationship. Hearing from you will probably make their day.

70. Find a freelance gig.

One way to fill up all of your extra time when you're feeling antsy and bored is by freelancing! From freelance writing to freelance drawing, to freelance social media jobs, there are tons of them out there that you can apply for.

71. Play putt-putt.

Don't let Covid keep you from being active. Try doing something sporty outside, like mini-golf that is safe and lets you social distance.

72. Listen to a Podcast.

You'd be surprised how entertaining Podcasts can be. There are ones out there that are about pretty much every topic under the sun so you won't have any trouble finding one you like.

73. DIY your own flower bouquet to display.

Spruce up your house with some flowers you arranged yourself! They'll look so good once you're done that your family will think you bought them.

74. Try a new Starbucks drink.

Starbucks is always coming out with new and fascinating flavors, so why not try some of them out? You can go through the drive-through or even have them delivered.

75. Paint or stain a piece of furniture in your home.

Being home may have you going stir crazy, so try upgrading some of your dull pieces of furniture. Painting, staining or even stenciling or your side tables or coffee table will give you the chance to be creative and makeover your space.

76. Teach yourself how to do a fishtail bread.

Thanks to YouTube and Instagram tutorials, you can learn how to style your hair like a pro! From fishtail braids to French braids to Dutch braids, the possibilities are endless.

77. Research the life of someone famous.

Sometimes the best thing to do when you're bored is to let yourself go down the rabbit hole of someone else's life. Once you start reading about their experiences online, the hours will fly by.

78. Decorate one of your white walls with washi tape.

Nail down a washi tape wall pattern you like on Pinterest and then map it out on one of your walls. Putting it on the wall behind your TV or bed will transform your space. Plus, if you get tired of it, you can always change it up later on.

79. Go to a park you've never been to before.

Getting outside and exploring a place you've never been is a great way to clear your mind and keep you from going crazy in your home. You can bring a book to read on a park bench, enjoy the nice weather or just sightsee.

80. Learn a TikTok dance.

You'll have hours of fun learning all the choreography to these catchy 15-30 second dances. You can even make up your own and challenge others to learn your moves.

81. Go through a drive-through and pay for the meal of the car behind you.

Sometimes you can feel like you're in a slump when you're stuck in your everyday routine. Change things up by going through a drive through and making someone's day by paying for their food. It'll be nice to do something kind for someone else, even though you're doing it at a distance.

82. Have an online cocktail party with your friends.

Get together, without leaving your house by setting up a Zoom cocktail party. You and your friends can even dress up so it'll be like you're out for a girls' night.

83. Teach yourself how to juggle.

You're never too old to learn a new party trick. So while you're stuck at home and trying to figure out what you can do when you're feeling bored, pull up a YouTube video that teaches you how to juggle. Start by mastering juggling a couple of balls and then keep adding more into the mix.

84. Pet sit.

Apps like Rover can change your life for the better if you're pet-less, but love animals. You can set up a profile and start pet sitting while you're hanging out at your house.

85. Clean out your fridge.

Let's be real: most people ignore how the inside of their fridge looks or try to avoid dealing with it altogether. But if you purchase some organizing bins off Amazon, you can make yours look like a celeb's!

86. Take an online cooking class.

If you have never had time to take a cooking class before, now you do! Sign up for a MasterClass cooking class and you'll be a chef before you know it! And if you're someone who already enjoys cooking, this will help you up your game in the kitchen even more.

87. Go on an online shopping spree.

Shopping is always a great way to pass the time. From Amazon to Macy's, you can hit up all of your go-to spots without using any gas.

89. Clean out your emails.

Sit down and de-clutter your emails one afternoon. To make things easier, do some sections at a time. If you want to go the extra mile, you can even start putting some of the emails you want to save into folders.

90. Dress up and take a family photo.

You don't need to go to a fancy photo studio to get a family portrait taken. In fact, since you and your family are all home with no distractions, take advantage of your extra free time and snap a new one. Pick a color for your family's outfits or pick a theme for everyone to follow and then select a pretty space outside that will provide a great backdrop. Then, set up your camera's self-timer while it's on a tripod and snap as many photos as you'd like.

91. Learn calligraphy.

By the time Christmas rolls around, you'll be glad you used your free time during quarantine to learn calligraphy. It'll be a great skill to have that you otherwise may have never had been able to pick up.

92. Stargaze and see what constellations you can spot.

Believe it or not, you can get bored from watching TV every single night. Switch things up and do a bit of stargazing one night instead. It'll be relaxing and enjoyable.

93. Detail your car.

If you want to save some money and make your car look brand new, detail your car. Just Google some hacks and tips on how you can do it yourself and then buy whatever products you need off of Amazon.

94. Go for a hike.

Being outside can do wonders for your mental health. Taking a hike (big or small) can be something you can do alone or with a friend. Plus, once you get to the highest point and see the view, you'll wonder why you hadn't started hiking before.

95. Have a tea party.

Change things up and host a tea party for you and your kids at home or a virtual one with your friends. You can include unique tea flavors, cute cookies and little sandwiches to munch on.

96. Make a time capsule with your family.

Your kids will love this activity! You can gather up items from around your house to put inside a treasure chest and then bury it somewhere in your backyard.

97. Make homemade ice cream.

In case your favorite ice cream shop isn't open right now or you don't feel safe going out and about, bring your favorite ice, cold treat to your house instead. Find a recipe online and make it in the morning so you can enjoy it in the afternoon.

98. Hang a gallery wall.

Putting one together may seem like a hard DIY project, but it's actually not. All you need are several different-sized picture frames and then a mixture of personal photos and scenic photos. Before you hang them up, arrange them on the floor in different ways until you find the perfect setup.

99. Watch a Broadway show online.

Take a break from your movie watching and watch a Broadway show at your house instead. It'll make you feel like you're in the theater and out of your living room, especially if you change into some nice clothes and make it into a special evening.

100. Get your karaoke on in your living room.

If you've been missing having karaoke nights at your favorite bar, bring the music to your house. Your family will have a blast belting out their favorite songs in your living room. You can even Zoom some family friends so they can be involved, too.

CHAPTER FIVE

50 most boring things in life?

people who Instagram their meals and Ed Sheeran have been voted among the nation's top 50 most boring things.

And the average Brit is bored for over three hours a day - adding up to more than NINE years of their life, a study has found.

Work is one of the most common sources of boredom, with 22 per cent of respondents bored for up to two hours - or 25 per cent - of their working day.

The survey of 2,000 adults in the UK was commissioned by online gaming company Casumo.com, whose spokesman said: "Boredom can be a real problem for many people, even if they're happy with their lives in general.

"Boredom can sap productivity, and make people feel like there's nothing good going on in their lives.

"We were surprised to find that people are more likely to feel bored at home than they are at work, and perhaps this shows a lack of imagination on the nation's part, that they can't entertainingly fill their free hours."

Being stuck in traffic emerged as the most boring thing about modern life, aggravating over half of the nation.

A slow internet connection, listening to drab football pundits‘ analysis and cleaning the house also appeared in the list of the most boring things in life.

As did PowerPoint presentations, the Kardashians and unnecessary work meetings.

THE 50 MOST BORING THINGS IN LIFE

1. Being stuck in traffic

Things to do While You're Stuck in Traffic

Whether you like it or not, it's happened to you, and it's most likely going to happen again. Getting stuck in traffic is like a rite of passage for all drivers out there, especially if you've taken the 401 in Ontario or Highway 40 in Montreal. It can be due to construction, weather, a collision or simply because of traffic in general; but one thing's for sure: it can be pretty boring.

CARFAX Canada understands this, and we want to help. Now, we can't stress this enough: this is for when either you're a passenger, or if you're pulled over to the side of the road, out of the way of other cars/traffic – the last thing we want is a distracted driver. Here's a handy list of things to do to pass the time; hopefully you don't have to do them all in one sitting.

Look, we're not Adele, or Seal, or Cher, or Beyoncé. But that doesn't stop us from belting out tunes. Plus, it may not be scientifically proven, but your voice sounds better when you're stuck in your car.

You look in front of you, the plate reads: AABB 123. What does it stand for? Always Avenging Beakless Birds? Or maybe it's Angry Antelopes Bathe Briskly. Either way, it's a good way to pass the time, and probably get a few laughs.

This one is much easier, and better, with a buddy. Without making it look like you're trying to, see if you can not only catch your traffic-jam-neighbour's attention, but also make them laugh. Bonus points if they roll down their window to ask what you're doing.

Whether you're listening to music, or already have a podcast playing, try starting a new series. Who knows, you might stumble across one you absolutely love, or you might find one that you can argue with. Either way, it will definitely pass some time.

There's probably a good chance that there's some trash or food that can be scooped up and tossed in a bag. The real trick is to remember to throw that bag out and not let it sit and become the garbage itself.

Most likely you don't have dumbbells or tension bands handy in your car, but that doesn't mean you can't do some exercises. Clench your abs, stretch your wrists or do arm circles. You can probably pair doing arm circles with the third tip on this list and be successful at both! #lifehack

This one pretty much needs a buddy. It's a classic car game that, so long as you're not sitting beside two wheat fields, it can eat up a good amount of time.

Another that requires at least one other person. Players have 20 chances to guess the person, place or thing you're thinking of. Pro tip for the competitive types: stray off the beaten path and choose car brands or celebrities that nobody has really ever heard of; the people you're playing with probably won't be too happy, but you'll for sure win!

Misery loves company! Call a friend or family member you know that you can chat hands-free with for the duration of the traffic jam. It's always good to catch up with people!

Bust out your Karaoke chops

Play the license plate abbreviation game

Make the person/people in the car next to you laugh

Switch it up with a podcast

Clean up the general area around your seat

Do some car exercises

Start a round of I-Spy

Become a champion of 20 Questions

Phone a friend

Nobody wants to be sitting in a traffic jam, but hopefully, with these tips, you're able to at least make the best of it. The most important tip of all though: pay attention to the traffic around you! The games and advice may be fun to do, but driving is always your top priority.

5 THINGS YOU CAN DO TO MAKE TRAFFIC JAMS LESS BORING

Traffic Jams. Whether you are a driver or not, it's safe to say that we have all been stuck in traffic jams at some point in our life. If you get stuck in this string of stationary cars on a daily basis then I feel extremely sorry for you.

Traffic jams are incredibly boring. You want to get to your location (sometimes there is added time pressure) and you are just not in the mood to be at a complete standstill on the motorway. Thankfully, I have some tips on how to make a traffic jam much more interesting...

Remember: These suggestions must not act as a distraction for you. You must always maintain concentration when driving on the road.

#1 - MUSIC

Music is a great way of curing the symptoms of boredom during a traffic jam. My suggestion for this is you make a playlist of songs you want to listen to during traffic jams so that you are prepared for the worst.

Another great thing to take advantage of is new music. There are so many genres of music out there that you may never have listened to before. Use the time you are spent stationary to listen to a new genre or artist, you may end up discovering a new favourite of yours!

The radio is another way of surviving traffic jams. Some find the radio dull, but if you enjoy the interaction the radio offers by playing along in the car; you may find yourself moving in no time!

As you can see, Apple promotes new artists or popular artists for you to try every day! Spotify, Amazon and YouTube Music are also great alternatives.

As you can see, Apple promotes new artists or popular artists for you to try every day! Spotify, Amazon and YouTube Music are also great alternatives.

#2 - PODCASTS

I always wanted to get into podcasts, but found I would turn them off after a few minutes to listen to my music instead. Recently, however, I started listening to 'On the Marbles', an F1 podcast made by Channel 4, and I have not turned back since. Infact, I wish they would produce them more often than every one or two weeks - that is how much I enjoy them!

If F1 isn't really your thing, then there are plenty of podcasts out there for you. For instance, the DriveTribe podcast is one setup by the staff of this very website! Apple Podcasts and Spotify are examples of platforms that have thousands of different types of podcasts for you to listen to. Whether you are into football, politics, or even anime; you can find nearly any topic you want.

Apple Podcasts is one of may great services fo find new content to watch!

Apple Podcasts is one of may great services fo find new content to watch!

#3 - JUST CHAT!

This requires two or more people to be in the car at once, but chatting is another great way to get through traffic jams. If you are one for debating, than have a debate with everyone! You will soon completely lose track of the time that you spent in the traffic jam as you go backwards and forwards discussing a controversial topic.

If you don't want to debate, then just chatting is absolutely fine. Find things to discuss, such as places you want to go to in the future, what is on your bucket list etc. Once again, just chatting will make the time fly by as you are away from the silence and won't be constantly checking the time.

#4 - CAR GAMES

When I was younger, I absolutely loved playing games in the car. If you are stuck with extremely bored young children in the car, then maybe 'I spy with my little eye' is something you can completely distract them with.

Nowadays, children tend to just use phones and tablets in the back seat to keep them occupied; but finding games to play with adults may make them feel more involved and spend more time away from their screens.

Whether it is counting colours of cars or searching for new registration plates, there is always a competitive aspect that will distract your children from the annoying question 'are we there yet?'

I played lots of car games when I was younger. Image: Nabeel Syed via Unsplash.

I played lots of car games when I was younger. Image: Nabeel Syed via Unsplash.

#5 - MAKE YOURSELF COMFORTABLE

There is nothing worse than being sat in an uncomfortable position when sitting in a car. Drivers and passengers can get out of the car after a long journey with back pains if their seats aren't in a position that is good for you. While this doesn't make the journey less boring; it makes the experience far more pleasant. Here is what you can do to make yourself more comfortable:

Put the seats back: Reclining your seat ever so slightly can help make traffic jams slightly more comfortable. Drivers should not move their seat far back enough to a point where their vision of the road ahead is affected.

Slippers: As a British person; I love slippers. Whenever I am a passenger in a long car journey, I always take my slippers with me in order to make my feet more comfortable. Instead of wearing shoes that are tight around your foot, soft slippers can make a huge difference. If there is one thing I could suggest, this would be it! This method should not be done by drivers.

Make sure the car isn't too hot or cold too! Image: Courtney Corlew via Unsplash.

Make sure the car isn't too hot or cold too!

Sleeping: Another passenger only suggestion (obviously). Sleeping has always been difficult for me in cars. However, you can buy travel pillows from shops in order to sleep more comfortably in the car. Sleeping is a great way to catch up on what you may have missed from an early start and can give you plenty of energy for when you arrive at your destination. This benefits the driver too, as they can pick any podcast or music artist they want!

2. Standing in line

Most of us experienced the grueling boredom of waiting in a line. Not only are lines boring, they can also be aggravating, and stressful. The New York Times explains why we hate lines, and what we can do about them.

The basic idea is that when you're unoccupied, the wait in a line feels longer. In fact, research suggests that people overestimate how long they've waited in a line by 36 percent. Those estimates are often based on expectation. The New York Times explains:

Our expectations further affect how we feel about lines. Uncertainty magnifies the stress of waiting, while feedback in the form of expected wait times and explanations for delays improves the tenor of the experience.

Oddly, our feelings about a line aren't just based on expectations. Our perception of a line is often all about that final moment. If a line speeds up at the end, we remember the experience positively. If it slows down, we have a negative memory.

The other problem with waiting in lines is that we're more likely to make impulse purchases when we're bored. This is why supermarkets place tabloids, candy, and gum in the checkout lane.

Can you really do anything about lines? Not really, but the New York Times offers one final bit of advice for dealing with them:

The dominant cost of waiting is an emotional one: stress, boredom, that nagging sensation that one's life is slipping away. The last thing we want to do with our dwindling leisure time is squander it in stasis. We'll never eliminate lines altogether, but a better understanding of the psychology of waiting can help make those inevitable delays that inject themselves into our daily lives a touch more bearable. And when all else fails, bring a book.

If you find yourself getting peeved when you're waiting in lines, the New York Times article is worth a read, even though you can rarely do anything about wait times. Unless, of course, you want to convince people to let you cut in line.

3. Being on hold

I recently read a great analogy on what it feels like to call customer service today. Imagine being a child again and asked to do your math homework – a subject you're unfortunately not very good at. You end up procrastinating the task for as long as possible because deep down you know it will take much longer than expected, and somewhere in the process, you'll be throwing up your hands in frustration. Speaking to a live agent is amazingly similar to doing your dreaded math homework.

Calling customer support is an incredibly annoying task that often becomes overwhelmingly frustrating. First, you've got to find the correct phone number for your region, then you have to listen to the maddening automated system to navigate your way to the right department, and more often than not, you'll be stuck with some elevator music while you wait on hold to speak to an actual human.

In an effort to make this experience a little less frustrating we've constructed some ways that you can avoid hold time and get an answer to your question quicker.

Here are 5 tricks to follow:

1) Take Your Problem to Twitter

When people are stuck on hold, they often talk about it on Twitter. By resorting to Twitter you can publicly shame a company for forcing you to wait on hold. Be sure to include their handle and any popular (yet relevant) hashtags so it gets picked up by other Tweeters.

One hashtag we recommend is #onholdwith. Onholdwith.com is a site that scans Twitter for EVERYONE waiting on hold and categorizes them in real-time by company and industry name (magical). The site provides a quick dose of reality for anyone who believes their customer service line is operating flawlessly. Here's a great example of a Tweeter waiting on hold and ensuring her tweet is catalogued on the site:

I'm #onholdwith @axainsurance. #28minutesandcounting Absolutely ridiculous and wasting my time at work. Do you ever answer the phone?

— Nat Ilenkovan (@natilenkovan) December 28, 2016

If companies respond to your tweet (which they should) be sure to ask for a special offer to appease you for the inconvenience.

2) Pretend Like You Speak a Different Language

Ok, I know this is a strange one, but a little bird told me it actually works. Most large companies offer a second language option (in Canada it's French, in the USA it's Spanish). Go ahead and press the number for the second language.

At this point, you are transferred into a queue for that language. Just hit "0" a few times and you will get to a rep. They will answer in the language that you chose, but if you start speaking in English, and you don't tell the rep that you intentionally hit the opposite language, you may have saved yourself a ton of time! The call center workers are all bilingual and the wait times are almost always shorter for the queues that offer the less popular language option.

3) Jump on Live Chat – It's Instant

We phone customer service because we want instant gratification. If we email it will likely take 24 hours for a response if we search self-service but the question isn't commonly asked we'll hit a dead end, and if we tweet but the resolution requires a more in-depth explanation the rep will just tell us to call the contact center. At this point, you just need an answer and live chat might be the perfect medium for this kind of support.

Of course, you'll need access to your computer or phone, but you'll likely experience a quick resolution with the added benefit of a conversation log, which you can't get after a phone conversation. The problem with chat is that if you hit a roadblock, and the agent simply can't help you any further, it's back to the phone. The other problem is that you have to start all over again as most companies don't have a chat-to-voice escalation plan, but it's worth a try before the phone call is made! Unfortunately, the voice channel is a fail-safe route.

4) Get Customer Service to Call You

When you're forced to phone support because all other avenues have failed, and you have to squeeze the call in at 9:00 AM on a Monday, chances are you'll be waiting on hold. You may not even be angry about the issue you're phoning about, but because you're stuck on hold the rage just begins to build. However, today there are easy fixes to this common call center problem. Rather than forcing you to wait on hold, a call center could offer you a call-back. Meaning you have the CHOICE to either wait on hold or request to have an agent call you when it's your turn in line.

Call centers who do not offer this feature either don't see it as a priority, or they're operating on old software that doesn't allow them to use this modern solution. However, they might not realize that even though their call center is on a legacy platform, they can still utilize the benefits of today's call-back solutions – so there's really no excuse not to offer this feature. In fact, if the organization doesn't offer you a call-back it's a clear representation of how they value your business.

5) Time Your Call

Although there's no single best time to call a contact center, there are some days and times that you could avoid if the call is not urgent. Mondays and Fridays in a call center are almost always busier. Meaning more people are phoning on those particular days, especially if the call center is closed on the weekend. It's also more likely that staff are absent on Mondays and Fridays.

In terms of timeframes, the period between 10 AM to 12 PM always tends to be busier. It makes sense too; people at work are calling during their breaks, parents are calling after dropping their children off at school, etc. You can expect "higher than normal" hold times during these periods, so if you can avoid it, why not?

Surveys regarding customer service dissatisfaction consistently show that waiting on hold is a top complaint. Hopefully, these tricks make the task a bit more pleasant, or the call center is smart enough to use call-back technology.

4. Junk mail

Junk mail refers to things we receive in the post but did not request, i.e., unsolicited mail. We use the term when referring to physical and electronic mail. Direct mail and direct marketing firms send junk mail to hundreds of millions of people across the world every week.

Companies use this type of mail to introduce new products, magazines, and investments. Local restaurants and businesses that deliver meals also send unsolicited mail to residents nearby. Charities send letters to people requesting donations.

In the advanced economies, such as the US, Canada, Western Europe, Japan, and Australasia, physical junk mail is a massive business. 'Physical,' in this context, means mail that we can touch; in envelopes. In other words, mail that comes to our front door.

In fact, most national postal services today would probably struggle to survive without junk mail. It is a lifeline for them.

Since the advent of the Internet, emails, and electronic communication apps, people have used traditional mail considerably less.

Traditional mail means physical mail, i.e., sending letters in physical envelopes with stamps, and using postal workers to deliver them, etc.

Today, most of us communicate online, either in writing, speaking, or video-conferencing. We even pay most of our bills and do our banking online.

However, we still receive physical mailshots in large numbers. A mailshot is a dispatch of mail, usually promotional material, which is sent to many people at the same time. Mailshots are a type of junk mail.

Merriam-Webster has the following definition of the term:

"Unsolicited mail that consists mainly of promotional materials, catalogs, and requests for donations."

Junk mail vs. spam

There are two terms – junk mail and spam – which have very similar meanings, but which we use in different situations.

Spam

Spam also refers to sending unsolicited letters to many people. However, spam only occurs online. You might receive spam via email, chat applications such as WhatsApp, Skype, and social media websites.

Companies, political parties, charities, and other entities use spam to promote their products, ideas, or raise money.

Sometimes, people send spam for sinister reasons. Perhaps they want to infect your computer with malware or a virus, steal money from you, or embarrass you. Malware, made up of the first half of malicious and the second half of software, is software that a programmer has deliberately designed to be harmful.

Spam is also a brand of canned cooked meat that Hormel Foods Corporation sells. It consists of pork, ham meat, salt, water, potato starch, sugar, and sodium nitrite.

Junk mail

Junk mail refers to unsolicited mail that companies, charities, political parties, and other entities send. However, unlike spam, the term may refer to either traditional or electronic mail.

In the early days of the Internet, we used the term extensively when talking about unsolicited electronic mail. However, 'spam,' appeared and started taking over.

Today, the term 'spam' dominates when talking about things in the digital world. We still see the word 'junk,' online. For example, in many email applications, there is a 'junk' folder, i.e., a folder for junk mail.

No one likes getting unwanted emails. These so-called spam emails can carry threats such as malware while receiving messages from unknown senders is just annoying!

According to Statista, spam messages accounted for 45.1% of email traffic generated in March 2021. In 2020, roughly 306.4 billion emails were sent on a daily basis, including billions of marketing emails.

Pro tip: To keep your inbox secure, you might want to use a cybersecurity solution like Clario. Clario's Safe Browsing feature is designed to detect fraud, phishing, and spam. Give it and other Clario tools a go by downloading a free 7-day trial (no credit card needed).

Promotional messages may seem harmless at first but too many may flood your inbox, especially if you receive them all the time. Malicious emails may also contain hazardous links or software too. Once opened, they can activate and infiltrate your device.

To prevent this from ever happening, we'll teach you the best ways to block unwanted emails in your computer or from your email provider.

Before we try to remove them from our inbox, let's learn more about the most common types of unwanted emails:

Spam emails: Also known as junk mail, most spam messages are sent in bulk to a list of subscribers, usually for promotional purposes.

Forced or accidental subscriptions: When using a new app or website, the service may use certain tactics to confuse you into agreeing to receive messages from them.

Phishing emails: These malicious messages pretend to be marketing emails but contain software capable of stealthily installing themselves on your device. The malicious software can then spy on your activities and even gather personal information about you. This can later be used for particular online crimes, including identity theft.

Emails with no sender: Known to iOs users as ghost emails, these "no sender" and "no subject" emails may actually be a result of a system glitch.

Unwanted personal communications: These are messages sent to you by someone you personally know, of which you have no intention of replying to. Maybe it's an acquaintance asking for a loan or a past lover still trying to reach out. Either way, they're cluttering up your inbox.

Why am I getting unwanted emails?

Why does anyone get spammed? Good question. Here are the most common reasons why:

You accidentally subscribed to a company's newsletter.

You have posted your email address on a public forum or website.

A company with details of your email was a victim of data breach.

You have previously clicked on a malicious email.

How to avoid getting unwanted emails

Here are some handy tips to prevent receiving unwanted emails in the first place...

Read the fine print of apps and websites' Terms and Conditions.

Maybe you're checking on the auto-subscribe option of these tricky text boxes.

Only subscribe to trusted companies or websites.

If you do willingly want to get newsletters and other promotional messages, make sure these are from trusted brands. Reputable companies do not spam their subscribers and are less likely to be involved in data breaches.

Don't engage with spammers.

Maybe you will be tempted to reply to these spammers to get them to stop sending you messages. However, it is usually best to avoid provoking them.

Use a disposable email.

Another technique tech-savvy individuals adopt is to use another email address when they sign up to new websites. This is called a disposable email and unconnected to your personal accounts. When its security is compromised, you can simply abandon this email address and it doesn't pose a risk to your other online accounts.

Don't reveal your private email address on public domain websites or social media groups.

Bots, spammers, and scanners, are always on the lookout for email addresses readily available online. If you still want to post your email address on social media, you may want to limit who can see it to select contacts.

5. Slow internet connections

There are many reasons your Internet connection might appear slow. It could be a problem with your modem or router, Wi-Fi signal, signal strength on your cable line, devices on your network saturating your bandwidth, or even a slow DNS server. These troubleshooting steps will help you pin down the cause.

Narrow Down the Problem With Multiple Websites and Devices

If your speed test confirms your internet is slow, you should try connecting to multiple websites and using multiple devices in your home if your Internet connection is slow. If the slowness is just with one website, it's probably that website's problem—not your internet's. There's not really anything you can do about this except wait for the people in charge of the website to fix it.

Narrowing down where the problem lies will help you fix it. Does the slowness just happen on one computer, or all your devices? If it's just one computer, you know the solution probably lies there. You may just have to reboot the computer, or you may need to perform a malware scan with your preferred antivirus to check that everything is fine. If the slowness happens on multiple devices—multiple computers, for example, or your computer and your phone—then it's almost certainly a network problem, and you'll have to go to your router.

Before going through a bunch of troubleshooting on your end, it's worth running a speed test using a website like Speedtest.net to see how well it's actually performing. Be sure to stop any downloads, uploads, Netflix streaming, or other heavy internet activity before running the test to ensure as little interference with the results as possible.

Compare the measured speed results against the expected speed of the Internet connection you're paying for. If you don't know this, there's a good chance you can find it on the bill for your Internet connection or your Internet service provider's website.

There are some caveats here. Speed tests may sometimes appear rather high, as some Internet service providers may prioritize them and they may have servers very close to you. If your connection speed appears a bit low, that can be normal—you generally pay for "up to" a certain speed and you don't always get the exact speed you pay for. Speeds may also be slower at busier times of the day, when everyone in your neighborhood is using the Internet connection, than at off hours when many people are sleeping or at work.

Of course, it could also just be that you pay for a very slow internet plan—in which case you'll need to call your internet provider and pay more to upgrade your service!

However, if you're paying for a certain connection speed and consistently receive speed test results that are well below that, it's time to move to the troubleshooting steps below.

Reboot Your Modem and Router

Like computers, modems and routers sometimes get stuck in a bad, slow, overloaded state. This problem can be fixed with a reboot. If you haven't rebooted your router and modem in a while, you should do it now.If you have a combined modem/router unit, you may just have one device to reboot. But there's a good chance you need to reboot two pieces of hardware: the router and the modem. The router connects to the modem, which is connected to the cable coming out of the wall. To reboot them, unplug each from their respective power outlets for ten seconds before plugging them back in. It may take a few minutes for your modem to reconnect to your Internet service provider and bring your Internet connection online, so be patient. Check if your speed improves after the reboots.

Improve Your Wi-Fi Signal

It's possible your internet is fine, but your Wi-Fi—which connects you to the internet—is having signal problems. A bad Wi-Fi connection can seem like an Internet connection problem, especially since it can affect all the devices in your home. There are quite a few reasons you may have a bad Wi-Fi signal. The airwaves could be congested with too many devices nearby, especially if you're using 2.4 GHz and not 5 GHz, which can support a lot more devices. This is a particularly common problem in denser urban areas—for example, if you live in an apartment complex with neighbors who have a bunch of wireless routers and other devices.

You could also just have a dead zone, something interfering with your Wi-Fi signal, or poor converage throughout your home. Consult our guide to speeding up your Wi-Fi and getting a better signal for more tips.

If you have a larger home or yard and need better Wi-FI coverage, consider getting a mesh Wi-Fi system that provides multiple base stations you can place around your home or property.

Your Internet connection is shared by all the devices in your home, so other devices on your network could be saturating your Internet connection, slowing things down for everyone else.

For example, if two people are streaming Netflix and one person is trying to download a file with BitTorrent, everyone's experience will slow down. Stop (or slow down) some of those other downloads to speed things up.If this is a particularly frequent problem, you may have to upgrade your internet package. However, you can also see if your router has a Quality of Service (QoS) feature, which will allow your router to automatically manage and assign how much bandwidth different devices and services receive. For example, it can automatically throttle BitTorrent bandwidth to avoid slowing down Netflix streams.

Check for Coax Splitters

If you have cable Internet and you have coaxial cable splitters on the line going to your cable modem, these could be degrading your signal strength and leading to slower Internet connection. Splitters vary in quality, and a bad, cheap one could lower your signal strength much more than a higher quality one would. A large number of splitters could cause a problem, too.

If you do have splitters on your cable line, try disconnecting them to troubleshoot your Internet connection. See how your Internet connection performs without any splitters on the line. If you have a much faster Internet connection speed, you've found your problem.

6. Listening to politicians

Does politics have to be a turn-off? The Observer asked a range of people from the media, the creative industries and non-party politics for ideas about how politicians and the media can re-engage voters. You can join the online debate here.

Sun 3 Feb 2002 01.18 GMT

"The government patently have little time for parliament, seeing it as a tiresome irrelevance. The third way was always meant to take the politics out of politics in favour of a business-friendly consensus. Is it any wonder the public view our toothless and subservient politicians with disdain? People hunger for energy and passion in their politicians. All we have at present are weary bureacrats".

- Rory Bremner

"People are clearly passionate about health, education, transport and other core policy issues. But they won't reward simplistic political promises and good-guy-bad-guy coverage with either votes or media loyalty. If the information on which people base their democratic choice is flawed as it is now - overspun and overhyped on both side of the political and journalistic divide - apathy is neither surprising nor wrong. Media and politics should hold a summit, call a truce, and re-draw the ethical lines of realistic political debate, and realistic political reporting".

- Julia Hobsbawm, Chief Executive of the public relations company HMC

"People are not bored with politics. What they are bored with is the tired way in which politics is too often presented to them by both the politicians and the media. The best political programmes have good, growing and appreciative audiences. The Observer, amongst other broadsheets, put on circulation during the last election, even though it was not one of the most stimulating or closely fought contests in recent times. And at the risk of sounding a slightly immodest note, there is a great appetite for reading about how we are governed. It is even possible to get a top ten best-seller, in both hardback and paperback, out of a book about government.

Politics succeeds in engaging people when the issues are vividly explored, the personalties are projected in a way which is compelling, and the dilemmas and dramas are made to matter.

It should not beyond the wit of the rich amount of talent there is in both politics and the media to switch people on again. Look at the great recent success of television series devoted to historical subjects. And what is history but the politics of dead people? If the dead can be made to come that alive for so many people, then we should be able to do it for the living".
- Andrew Rawnsley, Chief Political Correspondent, The Observer

"'Big P' Politics turns people off, but 'small p' politics doesn't. The trick is that people can be political, but disengage from 'Politics'. Much in the same way that friends reunited has re-connected people with people they used to know, someone needs to come up with an 'issues reunited' to link those seeking to be political - to protest, moan, or act - with others who might want to do the same. We must accept that this type of quick and sometimes dirty political engagement is much more likely to interest people than the life-times devotion to affairs of state which Politicians seem to want".
- James Crabtree, iSociety, The Industrial Society and Director, Voxpolitics

"Politics today seems so abstract that most young people fail to see a connection between their everyday lives and the suits stood bickering at the ballot box. If you want to get teenagers interested, make politics relevant; don't talk about the possible, highlight the actual. Champion clear and committed youth policies and stop using 'teenager' as another word for no good, socially dysfunctional layabout - they may not be eligible to vote now, but they will be one day. Follow the Yanks and enlist the help of stars to get young people listening. And pray that sometime soon a few impassioned politicians cut from the same cloth as Tony Benn come along and prove that not all MPs are in it for the perks and the glory".
- Helen Bazuaye, Editor, J17 Magazine

"Politics has entered an era of near constant electioneering the shrill tone of so much political debate has nullified the message (if any). The reason people have lost interest is that the level of debate is consequently at an all-time low. Politicians (egged on by an agenda-inebriated media) are too busy scoring points to forward any solutions beyond hollow pledges on everything from the NHS to the trains - two subjects the coddled political classes are uniquely ill-equipped to debate".
- Bill Prince, Deputy Editor, GQ

"Politicians need to start addressing the issues people really care about - the environment, especially global warming, is near the top of the list. And the media have to stop portraying politics as men in suits squabbling in Westminster - nothing makes politics look less inspiring and motivating.

Increasingly politics isn't about governments and parties anyway; for many people, it's about corporate power. And while some people may be disillusioned with voting once every four years, many more are getting involved in another kind of politics - taking direct action to stop the corporations".

- Laura Yates, Greenpeace

"Politics is out of synch with a world which has radically changed over the past 20 years or so. People have had to become much more self-reliant, both at work and in our private lives. At work we are continually assessed and have to deliver. At play, the boot transfers to the other foot as Britain finally embraces a service culture and consumers make their voices heard when things are not up to expectation. But the world of politics still appears to live in the land of extreme overclaim and underdelivery.

Of course, running a country is a hugely complex and difficult task. But credibility problems arise when the issues behind a failure to deliver are glossed over, rather than properly addressed. This eats away at the perceived competence of government to do anything other than 'talk the talk.' Most of the electorate have lost faith in New Labour's ability to improve the nation's quality of life. The answer is not to set out even more taxing goals and ambitions, but to look at the underlying causes behind the prevailing mood; to find the confidence to own up to being human and to acknowledge properly that it is finding things much harder than they actually appeared in May 1997. The government has the talent to turn the situation around. The question is whether or not they have the honesty and humility."

- Stef Calcraft, Director and founder, creative agency Mother

Preposterously, politicians pretend they'll fix everything. Predictably, they don't. Not because they don't try, nor because they're venal self-serving plutocrats; but because social problems are hard to fix. Consumer brands (despite their image in some quarters as the devil with a logo) are actually quite clever when it comes to promoting social change, and creating mass trust. They experiment. They listen. They respond to people's concerns. And crucially, they deliver what they promise: nothing more, nothing less. That has made brands the most trusted instutitutions in

contemporary society. Forget "rebranding" politics; forget making the voting process easier - that's just an infantilisation of the electorate. Politics should learn from brands about trust.
- Steve Hilton, partner at social marketing agency Good Business and former Tory campaigner.

"In a media society, debates about policies and ethical dilemmas only acquire a real existence when they appear on TV bulletins or in editorial pages. The media doesn't simply report on what our elected representatives do - it provides the spaces where citizens can scrutinise our representatives and hold them to account. If people are turning-off, the media is at least an equal culprit in the hollowing-out of our political culture.

But we have a shallow debate between those who think politics is boring and should be scaled back, and those who think it should be force-fed to a reluctant nation. The real problem is that covering politics as an inferior form of entertainment far removed from everyday lives, focusing on obscure personalities and Westminster wobbles rather than holding policies and decisions up to scrutiny and examining their impact on our lives.

Global issues are increasingly central to politics, yet foreign news suffers particularly at the hands of broadcasters. On one level, other countries seem to be on a different planet. In the age of the internet and cheap travel, programmes like "From our own correspondent" conjure up images of a white man on a voyage of discovery in the jungle. Yet foreign news also assumes specialist knowledge, and excludes those who don't already know about India's BJP or the political dilemmas facing President Megawati: it doesn't stop to explain why these issues matter.

Contrast the the innovative, informed coverage of science on television news. The discovery of the Human Genome was explained in well-thought out stages on peak-time national bulletins. Genes and DNA were couched in language an eight year old could understand; the medical applications were explored; the ethical dilemmas outlined. If journalists had reported in the style they usually reserve for politics, they would have focused solely on a horse-race between the US and UK research teams, complete with in-depth biographical information and a dash of incomprehensible scientific jargon".
- Mark Leonard, Director, The Foreign Policy Centre

7. Watching TV adverts

Global advertising spending reached more than $330 billion in 2019. And while companies continue to pump money into their ad campaigns, there's still a daunting obstacle blocking its path toward success: people's distaste for ads that are irrelevant to them and their interests.

According to HubSpot Research, 91% of people believe ads are more intrusive now compared to two or three years ago, and 79% believe they're being tracked by retargeted ads. So, it's not hard to imagine why people are pretty ad-averse these days. No one likes to feel like they're just another part of some secret algorithm, another cog in the advertising wheel.

Here at Wistia, however, we actually don't think advertising itself is the problem. It's not that all ads stink—it's just that the types of ads many businesses are running make people, well, cringe. We're not suggesting you give up on ads altogether, but we are suggesting businesses rethink the kinds of ads they're making, and ultimately, what they hope to achieve by running them.

Let's take it from the top—why do people dislike ads?

Think about the last time you researched a product you were considering buying online. Maybe you were on the hunt for the perfect pair of rain boots and ended up spending some time checking out a nice, sleek pair on L.L. Bean's website. Next thing you know, you're distracted by a notification on your phone. You open up the Instagram app, scroll the feed a bit, and then see an ad pop up from who else? L.L. Bean. The boots you were just checking out only a few minutes prior are now hanging out amongst photos of your friends and cute puppies.

Chances are you're either creeped out and annoyed by the ad or pleased to be reminded to go back and buy those beautiful boots. If we had to venture to guess, we'd say most folks fall into that first bucket.

Being followed around by a pair of shoes on the Internet for a few days is just one of the gripes people have with ads these days, but as it turns out, our aversion to ads has a lot more to do with psychology and our brain's chemistry than one might think. As a marketer, understanding what turns people away can help you make better ads that actually engage and delight your audience in new ways. Let's dig into the psychology behind why people hate ads so we can understand ourselves as humans a bit better!

"As a marketer, understanding what turns people away can help you make better ads that actually engage and delight your audience in new ways."

Ads feel like an invasion of privacy

As we just mentioned, retargeting can feel downright creepy and can easily rub people the wrong way when not done with care. The truth is, as humans, we don't like to feel like our behavior is being tracked and analyzed, even if it is common practice these days thanks to digital marketing. When it comes down to it, advertising can sometimes feel like an invasion of privacy, or in other words, an infringement on our personal space.

In fact, two neurologists at the University of Caltech discovered there's actually a structure in our brain that's responsible for telling us where the limits of our personal space lie, and that's the amygdala. The more time we spend online, the more the concept of personal space is translated from the physical to the digital. People want control over their own personal boundaries in their daily lives, and these days, that includes their online presence as well.

What you can do instead:

When ads feel way too personal, they can sometimes put people off from your product or service as a whole. Save retargeting for ads that promote your best, most valuable resources instead of hoping to just get your name out there with generic display ads. Once people give you an indicator that they want to hear more from you, whether they subscribe for a newsletter or watch a few videos on your site, you can feel more confident engaging with them again in the form of an ad that speaks to something they may be interested in learning more about (which isn't necessarily specifics surrounding your product or features).

Ads interrupt otherwise positive experiences online

Fast-loading websites and apps have conditioned us to crave instant gratification. We expect to get what we want and when we want it (which is usually, right now!). However, when surfing the web, digital ads get in the way of that goal, triggering feelings of frustration.

Can you recall a time where you were half-way through watching a video on YouTube or Facebook when a mid-roll ad pops up to just completely disrupt your experience? Yeah, we've all been there. Nothing's worse than ruining an emotional moment between you and a video of a dog being reunited with his owner than an advertisement.

What you can do instead:

Don't put your audience in an immediate state of distaste for your brand with a random advertisement that adds nothing to viewers' lives (and actually, takes away from it). Instead of slamming people with ads about your product, we recommend businesses try to build trust and good-will instead with engaging, creatively-driven content. How can you go about doing that with ads? Well, here at Wistia we think that adopting a Brand Affinity Marketing strategy is the best way to not only get people to know about your business, but to get them to actually like your brand.

Ads that aren't engaging, entertaining, or informative don't resonate with modern buyers

Many brands have caught onto the fact that these days, people make purchasing decisions based on the connections they have with the businesses themselves through the stories they tell and the values they uphold. What do companies like Rothys, Avocado, Warby Parker, Patagonia, and Everlane all have in common? They're devoted to their social missions, either as a core tenant of their business or just because it's the right thing to do, and they showcase those values through compelling storytelling online.

"Many brands have caught onto the fact that these days, people make purchasing decisions based on the connections they have with the businesses themselves through the stories they tell and the values they uphold."

Appealing to a niche audience and creating a positive emotional connection with them through storytelling is a far better use of those precious advertising dollars. Research shows that "...positive emotions toward a brand have a far greater influence on consumer loyalty than trust and other judgments, which are based on a brand's attributes." Old-school display ads that encourage people to "Hurry up and buy now before it's too late!" don't make people feel the warm-and-fuzzies. In fact, ads that are bereft of any value, whether that's in the form of entertainment or education, are a huge turn-off for folks who really care about the moral or ethical compass of the businesses they support.

What you can do instead:

We think businesses should lean into creative methods of storytelling through content and ads that actually create a strong emotional connection with viewers. And lucky for us marketers, creating a strong connection with your target audience (remember those Dove ads that left people in tears?) can result in tangible business benefits.

We experienced this firsthand here at Wistia with our original series, One, Ten, One Hundred. This was a docu-series we created that showcased the impact that constraints can have on creativity, and while we received a ton of qualitative love for the series, we also saw some quantitative indicators of success as well. While the average click-through rate for display ads is just 0.05%, 1.7% of the people who weren't already in our database and watched our video series created a free Wistia account. It just goes to show that with the right creative, you can make a connection with your audience and even turn them into customers (without making them angry).

Ads have started to all look and feel the same

Every day, more and more people experience banner blindness, which is a psychological phenomenon that essentially makes certain digital ads "invisible" to web users. This isn't a new finding by any stretch of the imagination—it's been well documented for over 30 years—and it isn't going anywhere anytime soon.

Ads these days tend to look and feel the same—remember how long the Tasty-style overhead shot was a novel concept? Not very long. The ads themselves are old and uninspired, and thanks to the abundance of best practices out there, they all look eerily similar. These ads are pretty boring, and it turns out us novelty-seeking human beings aren't fans of more of the same. Novelty makes us happy, and brain research has shown that a rush of dopamine accompanies fresh experiences of any kind, so just imagine what's happening in the brains of your audience when they see a banner ad from your competitor that looks just like yours? That's right...not much.

"Ads these days tend to look and feel the same. The ads themselves are old and uninspired, and thanks to the abundance of best practices out there, they all look eerily similar."

What you can do instead

According to research conducted by HubSpot, "A majority of our respondents agree that most online ads today don't look professional and are insulting to their intelligence." Pretty intense, right? Respondents in this survey not only think that most ads today don't look professional, but they also feel that obnoxious ads give people a poor opinion of the brands behind the ads themselves and the websites that allow them to be there in the first place. The moral of the story is that if you're going to run a bunch of ad campaigns, you might want to be sure to put some real effort into actually making them look and feel high-quality.

Turning a new page for advertising

As marketers, the way we market our products and services through digital advertising has to change if we want to see success. Beyond that, the way we think about what our audience actually wants from us also needs to evolve with the times. When you combine the negative perception of ads held by most with a cluttered web, the downfall of digital advertising becomes all too clear. Now that you know the psychology behind why people don't like ads, hopefully, you can set fourth down a new path that's more beneficial for all—one that aims to provide value to viewers and treats audiences like the humans they are.

Television was invented as a delivery vehicle for commercials. For years, viewers have been subjected to the onslaught of advertisers hawking their wares. Fortunately, with the advent of Personal Video Recorders or PVRs, viewers can skip the experience of commercials entirely. There are two ways to block commercials: one is by watching programs on a time delay and the other is by recording programs with the PVR and watching them later. A PVR with commercial blocking capability is required.

8. The routine of everyday life

First, let's define what routine means: A routine is a sequence of actions that you do repeatedly.

Brushing your teeth nightly and getting ready for bed is a routine. Waking up at 6:00 AM and exercising every morning is a routine. Purchasing a bagel and reading the news before you head to work every morning is a routine. Even eating chips while watching Netflix is a routine. They're all actions that happen again and again, a rhythm in your daily life.

That doesn't make them all good routines—they're simply routines by virtue of being done regularly. Helpful or not, every routine is powerful.

Routines Create High Achievers

We are what we repeatedly do. Excellence, then, is not an act, but a habit.

Aristotle

In his book Daily Rituals: How Artists Work, Mason Currey writes about the habits, routines, and rituals of hundreds of artists, including Frederic Chopin, Benjamin Franklin, Karl Marx, and Ernest Hemingway. Even though their routines varied wildly, each individual had steps they followed to put them in an optimal state of mind.

After studying the great artists, Currey came to this conclusion:

In the right hands, [a routine] can be a finely calibrated mechanism for taking advantage of a range of limited resources: time (the most limited resource of all) as well as willpower, self-discipline, optimism. A solid routine fosters a well-worn groove for one's mental energies and helps stave off the tyranny of moods.

Productivity guru and experimenter extraordinaire Tim Ferris has five morning rituals to get him into a productive state of mind: making his bed, meditating, exercise, drinking tea, and journaling. Performance coach Tony Robbins also uses a morning routine, which includes a cold shower, breathing exercises, and meditation to prepare him for each day.

High achievers tend to find routines that work for them and then stick to them—it's typically something they credit as a core to their success.

Habits vs. Routines vs. Rituals: Wondering what the difference is between habits, routines, and rituals? Habits are things that we do automatically--things like checking your email first thing in the morning or putting your keys in a specific spot when you get home. Routines are usually a collection of habits or actions you do on a regular basis to bring order to your day—checking your email, then writing your day's to-do list, then checking your team's project management tool as a way of getting the day started. Rituals are like routines. The main difference is the attitude behind the actions: Taking a walk everyday at lunch could be considered a routine if you think of it as something you need to do for your productivity. Or it could be a ritual if you think of it as a way to break out of the mundane and enjoy nature. While we're focusing on habits and routines here, most routines could be turned into rituals with a change of perspective.

Routines Put Our Brains on Autopilot

But what makes the routines of high achievers so powerful? As it turns out, we're creatures of habit and can use that to accomplish whatever we want. In The Power of Habit: Why We Do What We Do In Life and Business, Charles Duhigg details how habits put our brains into an automatic state where little or no willpower is required.

It works like this:

Step 1: Something happens that serves as a cue to your brain, putting it into "automatic" mode. A simple example is waking up. When I wake up, my brain immediately knows that it's time to turn on the coffee machine. This habit has been ingrained in my brain over years.

Step 2: Execute the routine. This is where I actually turn on the coffee machine, wait for it to brew, pour it into my favorite mug, sit in a chair by the kitchen window, and finally drink the coffee.

Step #3: Reap the rewards of the routine. The delicious flavor and high-octane caffeine reinforce the routine so that the next morning I repeat it again.

Making coffee is just one small routine, but the daily consistency of it helps keep me going. Imagine if other, more powerful tasks that can empower you to accomplish big things came as easy as making coffee?

This is the power of routines. The small repeated actions can have an exponential effect. By implementing routines in the morning and evening, you can prime yourself for maximum productivity each day.

Morning Routines to Help You Start the Day Off Right

If you win the morning, you win the day

Ferris's and Robbins's morning routines both include meditation, while the routines of many others include starting the day off with a fresh cup of coffee. Regardless of your morning schedule, here are some of the best ways to start your day and prepare for success.

Rise Early

There are exceptions, such as Winston Churchill who liked to say in bed until 11:00 AM, but many high achievers rise early in order to prepare for the day. In those early hours, they can execute their routines while the rest of the world is asleep.

Consider these examples:

Square CEO Jack Dorsey rises at 5:30 so that he can go for a six-mile jog.

Virgin Group founder Richard Branson wakes at 5:45 to exercise and eat a proper breakfast.

GM CEO Dan Akerson rises between 4:30 and 5:00 so he can talk to GE Asia.

Apple CEO Tim Cook gets up at 4:30 so he can send emails and be at the gym by 5:00.

Even if they aren't naturally morning larks--the opposite of night owls--they've trained themselves to wake up early for the many benefits an early rise can bring. Those include increased productivity with fewer distractions in the early morning, greater creativity because you can work when your mind is fresh, and less stress if you use that extra time for meditation or quiet contemplation. It could make you happier, too: Researchers in one study found that morning-type individuals reported higher levels of positivity and well-being.

Tip: Even if you're a night owl, you can train yourself to become a morning person by waking up 20 minutes earlier every day and soaking in some sunlight as soon as you wake.

Make Your Bed

If there's one habit you should adopt to improve your life, it's making your bed every day. That, at least, is the advice from Navy Seal Admiral William H. McCraven:

If you make your bed every morning, you will have accomplished the first task of the day. It will give you a small sense of pride, and it will encourage you to do another task, and another, and another. And by the end of the day that one task completed will have turned into many tasks completed.

Making your bed will also reinforce the fact that the little things in life matter. If you can't do the little things right, you'll never be able to do the big things right. And if by chance you have a miserable day, you will come home to a bed that is made — that you made. And a made bed gives you encouragement that tomorrow will be better.

It's all about the small things.

Recite Affirmations

Affirmations are positive statements you can use to reframe how you think about yourself and the day to come. They are a way of visualizing the good things that will come to you that day and overcoming negative self-talk.

In his book The Miracle Morning: The Not-So-Obvious Secret Guaranteed to Transform Your Life (Before 8AM), Hal Elrod says:

When you actively design and write out your affirmations to be in alignment with what you want to accomplish and who you need to be to accomplish it—and commit to repeating them daily (ideally out loud)—they immediately make an impression on your subconscious mind. Your affirmations go to work to transform the way you think and feel so you can overcome your limiting beliefs and behaviors and replace them with those you need to succeed.

Some simple affirmations you could use are:

I will do great things today

I will make $XXX this year

I am a highly respected [insert occupation]

I am achieving [big goal]

Your aim is to affirm and visualize the things you want to happen. As you focus on these things, you begin to believe that you can and will achieve them, which then enables you to take action on them.

Although it might sound New-Age-y to some, affirmations are proven methods of self-improvement. As clinical psychologist Dr. Carmen Harra says. "Much like exercise, they raise the level of feel-good hormones and push our brains to form new clusters of 'positive thought' neurons."

Get some exercise

There are few things more transformative than exercise. Exercising in the morning increases blood flow, releases endorphins, and strengthens your body. It prepares you for the coming day, increases your overall energy levels, and helps you remain in optimal health. Numerous studies have shown that exercise is key in fighting depression and anxiety, and a Finnish study suggested that exercise is even correlated with increased wealth.

Implementing a daily routine of exercise will prepare you for maximum success through the day. And it doesn't even have to be a full gym workout to reap the benefits: A brisk walk in your neighborhood, a 7-minute workout, or a quick yoga session could get you going.

Need more motivation to get moving? Try tracking your activity automatically with Zapier, an app automation tool. With logs of your runs or workouts, you can see your progress and challenge yourself to keep at it.

Eat a proper breakfast

The fuel you consume in the morning has a significant effect on your ongoing performance—and thus, it should be the best fuel possible.

Dietician Lisa De Fazio recommends staying away from high-sugar, high-fat breakfasts and instead suggests a healthier choice, perhaps:

Oatmeal

Low-fat breakfast sandwich

Smoothie

Fruit and yogurt parfait

Think good carbs and fiber plus some protein. Those foods will give you energy and satisfy your food cravings while setting the stage for good decisions all day.

Take a cold shower

This one may seem a little extreme, but many people swear by taking cold showers each morning. It's similar to athletes who take ice baths, although slightly less frigid.

Why a cold shower? Because it can increase blood flow, burn away unhealthy fat, and release dopamine into the body. Like exercise, it kick starts your body.

This is why Tony Robbins plunges into 57 degree water every morning. He's convinced that it is essential for maximum productivity.

These might seem like minor things--waking up early, making your bed, saying your affirmations, exercising, eating a good breakfast, and taking a cold shower--but taken together into one consistent routine you do every day, you're well prepped to face anything that happens after. A morning routine takes the stress out of the start of the day and puts you on the best footing from the get-go.

Of course, customize your morning routine for your own preferences. The SAVERS graphic above from James Altucher's article and podcast with Hal Elrod can help you remember a few other things you can add to your morning routine: silence, visualization, reading, and scribbling. For more inspiration, My Morning Routine offers 200+ examples of morning routines you can adapt and adopt for yourself.

Evening Routines That Set the Tone for the Next Day

The close of each day is just as important as the start. By implementing evening routines, you ready yourself for the next morning, recharge with a restful night, and minimize the resistance you encounter in getting things done.

Prepare goals for the next day

Determining your objectives for the coming day does two things. First, it allows you to identify your most important tasks in advance—before all the pressures of the day arrive on your doorstep. Ideally, the first few hours of each day should be spent conquering your most challenging task. This idea has been given various names, such as "eating the frog" and "slaying the dragon."

Second, it allows your brain to begin thinking about those tasks as you fall asleep. In their book Organize Tomorrow Today: 8 Ways to Retrain Your Mind to Optimize Performance at Work and in Life, authors Jason Selk, Tom Bartow, and Rudy Matthew say:

Identifying daily priorities might seem like an obvious or insignificant step to take, but writing your most important tasks down the previous night turns your subconscious mind loose while you sleep and frees you from worrying about being unprepared. You'll probably find that you wake up with great ideas related to the tasks or conversations that you hadn't even considered!

Reflect on the day's achievements

It can be easy to lose sight of victories after a long day. Taking just a few moments at the end of the day to reflect on and celebrate your wins puts things into the proper perspective and gives you encouragement for the coming day. It helps you overcome the discouragement that often comes with setbacks.

In addition to asking at the start of his day "What good shall I do this day?", Benjamin Franklin asked every evening "What good have I done today?".

Benjamin Franklin

Zen Habits author Leo Babauta puts it this way:

If you reflect on the things you did right, on your successes, that allows you to celebrate every little success. It allows you to realize how much you've done right, the good things you've done in your life.

You can do this in a variety of ways, including jotting things down in a blank Moleskine notebook, a gratitude journal, or an app on your phone. You can automatically track your productivity with RescueTime and Zapier as well:

Clear your head

It's easy to take your work to bed, making it difficult to fall asleep as you mull over job-related problems. Clearing your head before sleep allows you to put aside the challenges of the day and ready your mind to shut down. There are numerous ways to do this, including:

Meditation

Light reading

Playing Tetris (for productivity!)

Watching a peaceful television show (The Walking Dead probably isn't your best bet)

Doing a "brain dump" of all the thoughts in your head in a journal before you go to bed

Buffer CEO Joel Gascoigne describes his disengagement this way:

For me, this is going for a 20-minute walk every evening at 9:30 p.m. This is a wind-down period, and allows me to evaluate the day's work, think about the greater challenges, gradually stop thinking about work and reach a state of tiredness.

Your goal is to engage your mind in something completely non-work related.

Prepare for the next morning

In order to minimize the amount of thinking you need to do in the morning, take time to prepare things. Pick out the clothes you'll wear, prepare the food you'll eat, prep the coffeemaker, and organize any work related materials you need to bring. If you'll be going to the gym, lay out your workout clothes and water.

The less time and mental energy you expend on inconsequential things, the more you'll have for the things that matter.

Tidy up

Waking up to a messy home isn't the most motivating way to start your day. Without regular sessions cleaning up and putting things away, you'll find your place quickly in disarray.

Thankfully, spending just 10 to 20 minutes a night tidying up will help reduce stress in the mornings and help you avoid marathon cleaning sessions on the weekends. If there's only one thing you do,clean and shine your sink. Like making your bed in the morning, this one task will give you a sense of accomplishment. Housekeeping guru FlyLady says:

This is your first household chore. Many of you can't understand why I want you to empty your sink of your dirty dishes and clean and shine it when there is so much more to do. It is so simple; I want you to have a sense of accomplishment! [...] When you get up the next morning, your sink will greet you, and a smile will come across your lovely face. I can't be there to give you a big hug, but I know how good it feels to see yourself in your kitchen sink. [...]

Go shine your sink!

Also, if you have children, you know the importance of setting up solid routines with them. They can help out too!

Practice proper sleep hygiene

Very few people practice proper sleep hygiene and their sleep suffers as a result. Generally speaking, you should:

Stick to the same sleep and wake schedule.

Minimize blue light from screens (this can be done using F.lux on your computer and "Night Mode" on your mobile device).

Set the temperature in your room to between 60-65°F (15-18°C).

Make your room as dark as possible.

It can be easy to minimize the importance of sleep, but it's absolutely essential for optimum performance. In fact, sleep is so crucial that Arianna Huffington devoted an entire Ted Talk to it.

It can be really tough to build routines into your life. It takes intention and discipline. Sometimes it feels simpler to just get the day started and then after a long workday crash into bed.

But the good thing about routines and habits is that the more you do them, the easier they become. They become ingrained in your day to the point where you find it harder to not do them.

So stick with it. You may find it tedious at first, but you'll find your days will flow much more smoothly when you've bookended them with quality morning and evening routines.

To create your morning and evening routines, you can write up a checklist that you can walk through every day until it becomes ingrained in you or set up a schedule, a la Ben Franklin. For example:

6 AM: wake, make the bed, get coffee started

6:15: drink coffee and read the news

6:30: exercise

7: eat breakfast

7:15: shower

8-5: work

6: dinner

7:30: tidy up

8: time with family, TV, or other form of relaxation and entertainment

9:30: journaling or meditation

10: bedtime

What's your daily routine like?

9. Sitting in a waiting room

Waiting room boredom is real, and doesn't appear to be improving. Cartoonists and comedians have had much to say about the long wait times in the healthcare provider's office, and as is often the case, there is some truth behind these witticisms. A 2014 study found that the average wait time in a healthcare provider's office in the U.S. is 20 minutes, 16 seconds and getting longer.1 Until a solution comes along, if one can at all, we have a number of tips for making your time spent waiting not only tolerable, but perhaps even productive and/or enjoyable.

There are a number of reasons for long wait time, but that doesn't make it any less aggravating. Our waiting room survival activities are broken down into things that are enjoyable, practical, funny, or educational, with special tips on waiting with children. Finally, we will talk about why long wait times may occur, and why having to wait for a healthcare provider can actually be a good sign.

Enjoyable Activities

Instead of focusing on "losing" time, view your wait as an opportunity to do something you enjoy—something you wouldn't ordinarily do in a normal workday.

Take time to crack the spine of that novel you've been meaning to read. Don't worry that you aren't accomplishing anything (if you tend to be a doer). You are enjoying a few moments of pleasure that you deserve, and that's important!

Visit with another patient. Do you see anyone who looks lonely or anxious? Ask first, as the patient you notice may not wish to talk. On the other hand, it's surprising how fast a long wait time can slide by when you are taking the time to listen to someone who is lonely.

Bring a friend to talk to. It's not a coffee shop, but a healthcare provider's waiting room can actually be a good time to talk without interruptions—that is, unless your healthcare provider is on time.

Practical Activities

What are some activities that you dread and are always putting off? Using your wait time to address one of these chores not only makes the wait go faster but can free you up when you return home to your family. On the other hand, what are some things you would like to do (limited by the confines of a waiting room) but haven't been able to justify the time it takes (for example, playing with your phone)? Here are a few ideas:

Write a letter. Is there a letter you've been meaning to send but just haven't gotten around to? Pack stationary, cards, and your address book—even stamps so you can mail the letter on your way home so it doesn't get lost. Keep in mind that in this day of email, people still appreciate receiving snail mail cards and letters.

Balance your checkbook

Work on your taxes

Take a nap. First, let the receptionist know you may be sleeping so you don't miss your appointment.

Make a master to-do list. Make a list of household things that need to be done, purchased, or repaired. Or check for grocery list apps for the iPhone.

Do your daily devotional or a meditation

File and/or polish your fingernails

In a waiting room, a patient recently asked, "What is iCloud?" Even if you've forgotten to bring a book or writing materials you will usually have your phone. If you have a smartphone, learn how to use functions that you aren't familiar with, organize your email or photos into folders, or hunt for new and interesting apps.

Humorous Activities

If you are really bored, it may help to resort to some humor. Consider these ideas:

Bond with your children by observing other patients in the waiting room and comparing them to your favorite cartoon characters (do this discretely).

For adults, play with the toys in the children's section of the waiting room.

Search for funny memes and send them to family and friends.

Patient Education

Some researchers have proposed that waiting time wait times are actually an untapped opportunity. Unless you are being seen for a routine physical, you may have questions about your symptoms or those of a family member. Here are some ideas for using your wait time to support your physical health.

Make sure your medical history is accurate and updated. Some healthcare provider's offices will give you a sheet with current diagnoses and medications. While you wait you can make sure that the information is accurate (which often it isn't) so that it can be updated during your appointment.

For some concerns, you can ask if the office has questionaires. For example, many healthcare providers have questionaires about anxiety or depression. Filling these out while in the waiting room can save time later on.

Write out or review questions for your visit. Is there anything you can add? Sometimes when you are bored you may think of things you would otherwise overlook. You may also wish to write down your goals for your visit. If you do this, make sure to speak up and share this with your healthcare provider during your visit.

Ask the receptionist for patient education materials that you can review. Many offices have handouts on a wide range of medical conditions. Taking time to review these may help stimulate further questions you should ask.

What to Pack in Your Waiting Room Bag

If you only see your healthcare provider once a year, it's probably not worth the trouble of packing a waiting room bag. But if you happen to have several visits, for example, follow-up visits, consultations, second opinions, or chemotherapy visits, keeping a bag ready may ease the frustration of waiting. Consider packing some of these items:

The book you've been meaning to read. Make sure to pack a bookmark as well.

Your address book

Stationery and cards, stamps

Your favorite pen

Your knitting or crochet supplies

A lightweight blanket if you get cold

Crossword puzzles or sudoku

An iPod with headphones

Chargers for your phone/ipod/ipad

A water bottle and snacks. Choose snacks you can keep packed and ready such as granola bars.

Magazines: Yes, many waiting rooms provide magazines, though patient complaints about magazines are common enough that a 2014 study in the British Medical Journal addressed the issue. It turns out that the problem is not lack of new magazines, but the disappearance of new magazines from waiting rooms. If you like science, you don't need to worry. Disappearances were common for gossipy magazines (though the specific magazines weren't identified for fear of litigation), but not scientific magazines.2

Going through chemotherapy can mean multiple wait times along with side effects that require extra caution. Check out this essentials list of what to pack for chemotherapy.

Another reason to bring your own reading and writing materials is infection prevention, especially if you are immunosuppressed. In a 2017 study in Paris, researchers cultured magazines found in hospital waiting rooms. Along with normal skin bacteria, they found pathogens (bacteria and fungi that could potentially cause infections) such as Staphylococcal aureus, Enterococcus faecalis, Aerococcus viridins, and Aspergillus.3

Waiting With Children

Waiting with children can be much more difficult than waiting alone. Consider the appetite and attention span of the typical child. Many waiting rooms provide toys and books, but it can be helpful to pack your own bag. You likely know what activities will keep your child's attention the longest, and if it's during flu season, or if anyone in the family has an immune system that's suppressed, you may wish to avoid the germs that live on waiting room toys (though, surprisingly, toys and books in waiting rooms are less "germy" than one would expect). Here are a few ideas for items:

Handheld electronic games

Your phone (or theirs)

An iPad

Water or juice, healthy snacks such as granola or cut up fruit

Coloring book and crayons or colored pencils. (Buying a new coloring book or markers and wrapping them in pretty paper can make this extra special.)

Books

Small toys such as action figures

Play I spy. If you've forgotten how this goes, you say "I spy" and your child tries to identify what you are looking at. For example "I spy something that is green and loves water" (an office plant).

Why the Wait?

At first glance, you may ask why healthcare providers can't be on time—for example, as an attorney or accountant would be on time for an appointment. One of the problems is urgency. If you haven't finished going over your taxes, you can make another appointment in a week. Not so with a bloody nose, severe belly ache, or with a baby who chooses to be born at that moment. Unpredictability is another reason, especially in primary care. Receptionists schedule what they guess is an appropriate amount of time for an appointment. But when a headache could be related to mild seasonal allergies, or instead a brain tumor or stroke, this is a challenge.

It's sometimes even the case that a long wait time is a good sign. While it's not always the case, it could be that the healthcare provider who falls the furthest behind during the day is the one who is most compassionate and thorough. The backed-up healthcare provider may be choosing to let patients wait (something that leads to further delays as she needs to apologize to each later patient), and arrive home late for dinner, in order to give a patient the time she would want a family member to receive in the same setting.

Lack of time has been cited as the greatest barrier to practicing solid evidence-based medicine in primary care. And while it could be argued that healthcare providers should simply schedule more time with each patient, the chance that this is under a healthcare provider's control is uncommon in modern medicine, at least if a healthcare provider hopes to remain employed.

Getting upset about long waiting room wait times is unlikely to benefit your health, and is equally unlikely to change the system. Instead, being prepared and using your time in a way that helps you accomplish a task or at least enjoy your time might be just what the healthcare provider ordered. In so many situations in life, reframing—or looking at the same situation in a different Light—can sometimes actually make that same situation become a positive rather than a negative.

10. Queuing in the post office

Think Post Office and you more often than not think haphazard counters with long queues. Any work to be done at this offices have been linked to being tedious and cumbersome. However, this is now in for a huge change. Nisha Nambiar, in this article of the Indian Express, writes about a model Post Office being introduced in Baramati. This PO will boast installation of latest technology in addition to automated kiosks and electronic token systems.

Union communications minister Jyotiraditya Scindia had launched the project to upgrade and modernize 500 post offices in 10 selected postal circles in two phases. In the first phase, 50 post offices were identified for their physical appearance and for their work environment.

Jarodia, who will inaugurate the post office, said, "In the state circle five post offices have been identified for the first phase. Besides Baramati in Pune region, the others are Nanded, Bhandara, Calangute and Jawahar."

11. Having no money

13 Ways to Have Fun Without Spending Money

With a little creativity, you'll feel like a tourist in your hometown. And your wallet will thank you.

It's no secret that attending the hottest concert in town, hitting the newest club or catching a movie at the nearest theater can be expensive, and the cost of social engagements can really add up weekend after weekend. According to a survey from the Bureau of Labor Statistics, Americans spent an average of $2,913 on entertainment in 2016. Reducing your entertainment budget can therefore be an easy way to trim your spending and a simple way to save money.

Don't worry. Cutting back on entertainment costs does not mean saying goodbye to your social life. There are plenty of ways to have fun without spending money, and you don't have to look further than your own backyard.

“How many New Yorkers haven’t ridden the Staten Island Ferry or gone to a live concert in Central Park?” says Donna Freedman, a writer who focuses on personal finance.

Whether you’re facing a thin wallet this Friday night, or you just want to reduce your entertainment expenses in general, here are 13 fun things to do without spending money that will make you feel like a tourist in your own hometown:

1. Go on a picnic

A picnic with family or friends is a way to have fun without spending money, and you can go to your favorite outdoor spot or use it as an opportunity to explore someplace new. Emma Healey, a money-saving expert and founder of the blog Money Can Buy Me Happiness, has a specific strategy. She’ll pull up Google Maps and search for green patches near her home. Then, she’ll Google the name to see if it’s a place she can take her kids.

“Once we discovered a nature reserve hidden behind some farmland, with a trail through the woods and a rope swing for the kids at the end,” Healey says. “There was no one else there, so we enjoyed the forest all by ourselves and the kids thought it was the best thing ever.”

2. Go to no-cost museum and zoo days

If you have museums or zoos in your area, check out their websites to see if they offer days when you can visit without paying admission. The downside is that these days can be relatively popular and crowded, but it’s worth it if you’re trying to find fun things to do without spending money. Some companies also have deals with local museums that allow employees and their families to attend without cost on specific days, so check in with your employer to make sure you’re taking advantage.

3. Give geocaching a try

If you have a smartphone, chances are you already have all of the equipment you need for this hobby. It’s based on a simple idea: People have hidden more than 3 million treasure stockpiles (known as geocaches) all around the world, and it’s your job to find them using only a GPS. To get started, simply download the Geocaching app or log in to the Geocaching website. Bonus: This activity may bring you to local spots you’ve never visited, which is a way to be a tourist in your own hometown.

4. Leverage your chamber of commerce

Many towns and cities offer no-cost festivals, music nights and other events. This is an easy way to enjoy your hometown, socialize with friends and mix up your activities on evenings out—all without opening your wallet. To scope out upcoming events, check out the website for your local chamber of commerce for ways to have fun without spending money.

5. Take a historical city tour

Did you know that no-cost historical walking tours are available in many cities? For kids and adults alike, these tours are often put together by businesses, chambers of commerce or governments and are a way to be a tourist in your own hometown. To find out if one is available near you, search for "walking tour" on the website of your local historical society, city or chamber of commerce. Sometimes these tours are led by volunteers, while others are offered as self-guided tours.

6. Visit a farmers market

If you're a frugal foodie, farmers markets in your hometown can offer affordable, fresh produce, especially if you go at the end of the day when vendors are more inclined to offer discounts to get rid of extra merchandise.

But, to make this another of the many ways to be a tourist in your own hometown, why not try something new? Rather than getting your favorite vegetables, try challenging yourself: Pick out one to two vegetables you normally wouldn't buy, and then find a recipe for them. You'll save money by not eating out, and you'll increase your cooking repertoire.

You could still check out the farmers market and turn it into a nice walk or outdoor picnic if you're looking for fun things to do without spending money.

7. Go camping

A way to have fun without spending money is to find an outdoor adventure. While some campgrounds charge fees, it's also possible to find no-cost sites. You can camp on most national forest land for no cost, for example. It's called dispersed camping, but you may have to follow specific rules, such as being a certain distance from water sources and developed campgrounds.

Lest you think camping is a fun thing to do without spending money only for people living way out in the sticks, it is possible to find dispersed camping areas—as well as other campsites with minimal fees—near many large cities. For tips on recreational opportunities and how to visit public lands, it's a good idea to check with your local or regional Bureau of Land Management, U.S. Forest Service or State Parks office before heading out.

8. Do a photography challenge

Looking to boost your photography skills and explore hidden nooks and crannies as a way to be a tourist in your own hometown? Google "photography challenge" to find lists of things to take pictures of each day for a set period of time. Items like "find something red" and "take a picture of something abandoned and forgotten" can turn your photography into a real hometown treasure hunt.

9. Check out books from the library

Freedman, the author, says she uses the library all of the time as a way to have fun without spending money. "On the way out I always stop at the 'New Arrivals' section and scoop up new reading material," she says.

You might be surprised by how accommodating libraries are, even if your local branch is no larger than a walk-in closet. For example, if you're interested in reading something that you can't find on the shelves, most libraries are able to order it for you.

Many libraries are full of even more fun things to do without spending money, like checking out DVDs, cameras or binoculars.

In some locations, "you can get access to free passes to museums and other local cultural attractions," Freedman says.

Going to the library, versus downloading content on your devices, can also become an event in and of itself and an opportunity for the family to get out of the house.

10. Volunteer

You may not think of volunteering as a way to have fun without spending money, but there are tons of organizations in your area that can use your help right now. Ask at a local nonprofit, such as a food bank or a wildlife rehabilitation center, or use a website like VolunteerMatch to find opportunities. You could meet new friends, feel good about helping the residents of your hometown and even develop new skills.

11. Find a fun meetup group

Speak a foreign language? Interested in home-brewing beer? How about spelunking? Meetup.com provides a way to find other locals with similar interests. You could also find new places in your hometown to explore if you join a club that moves around, such as a running club or a home-brewing club that visits different breweries. Pro tip: You can carpool to activities with others in the group to save on gas.

12. Go bird-watching

Even if you're not a bird expert, with your checklist of all the birds you've ever seen handy at all times, this could be a new hobby and a fun thing to do without spending money. There are birds wherever you are (even in the biggest of cities), and all you need is a bird book and binoculars to get started. See how many birds you can spot in your hometown.

13. Take a hike

Hiking is a great way to see nature and get great exercise, even if you live in a large city. To find trails near you, check out websites like AllTrails, which provides detailed trail maps, trail reviews and crowdsourced trail photos. You can carpool with friends to save on gas and combine hiking with another fun outdoor activity like bird-watching or geocaching.

So many ways to have fun without spending money

Entertaining yourself and your family locally does not have to mean constantly spending money on events and outings. Sometimes it's the simplest excursions that are the most enjoyable and memorable. Whether you need to save a few bucks for the short term or rework your budget to focus on other priorities, these 13 examples of ways to be a tourist in your own hometown will help you find new and fun things to do without spending money.

12. Tidying up the house

You know you need to clean your house or apartment regularly. Yet many people put it off or don't bother cleaning at all. Next time you aren't motivated to clean your home, remind yourself of all the benefits on why it's important to regularly clean your home. Here are several to remember:

It helps keep you organized: Cleaning your home regularly helps keep you organized. You know where all your things are and don't waste time trying to find your keys or important documents.

Reduces stress: Not only is it stressful having to search for lost items, but not cleaning increases stress. Just looking at cluttered spaces is stressful. It reminds you of all the things you need to do and makes your home seem smaller than it actually is. Instead of worrying about how you never clean your living room, avoid stress by cleaning weekly.

It keeps you from collecting junk: By regularly cleaning your home, you get rid of unwanted papers, junk mail, and other items you don't need anymore. Don't let this stuff pile up – look through it every few weeks and get rid of what you can as soon as possible.

Reduces allergies: If your house or apartment isn't cleaned regularly, dust and other allergens will build up. Cleaning every week will help avoid allergies or other breathing problems.

Avoid spreading germs: Keeping your house clean will stop the spread of germs and help keep you healthy. Cleaning up spills, vacuuming your carpets, and keeping your kitchen and bathroom clean will kill germs. Avoid getting sick by cleaning your home.

Keeps out pests: Bugs and rodents are attracted to spills, food particles, and other sources of food. If you don't clean your kitchen, dining room, and other place you eat, you have a higher chance of having pests. Not only are pests unpleasant, they also spread germs and allergens.

These are some of the reasons to regularly clean your home. If you don't have the time or energy to keep your house clean, contact us today! We offer a variety of cleaning services and can help you keep your home clean.

You step into your room and stumble upon something hard that hurts you, you have to tiptoe your way to your bed because there is not enough space to walk, your bed has huge piles of clothing spread everywhere, your table groans under books, newspapers, cups, and all other kinds of stuff, and your closet looks like a ransacked outlet store post-Black Friday. If that's a common scenario for you, then you are living in a space that disrupts your ability to use it well.

Your room is the place where you start and end your day. Whether you are aware of it or not, the physical space in which you live and spend a lot of your time has an important role to play in how we behave. Having a bedroom in such a messed state can have a variety of effects on your life. Our mind cannot live completely independent from our environment; therefore, keeping the room tidy, organized, and clean is significant. A straightened room with a made bed and pile-free floor will not only bring happiness and organization to your life, it will also change your life!

1. You will know what resources you have

Do you find yourself looking everywhere for your matching bracelet or clothes when going for a party or out with friends? Or does it happen that you buy a pair of pants, only to find out later that you had a better one to match the shirt you were wearing to the event? Keeping your bedroom tidy will let you know what things you have – the shoes, clothes, jewelry, books, magazines, and stationary – that are among your belongings so that you don't have to rummage for them everywhere or go and buy new things when you already have better alternatives.

2. Your thoughts will also be tidied up

Tidying your place also tidies up your mind. It is suggested by psychologists that a messy room is a representation of a disorganized mental state. When one is tidy and organized it also builds into their life, helping them in everything.

As Marie Kondo states in The Life-Changing Magic of Tidying Up, "From the moment you start tidying, you will be compelled to reset your life. As a result, your life will start to change." So, if you want to bring a change to your life, go ahead with cleaning and organizing your space and start a tidying marathon.

3. Tidying your room can save you time

Tidying your room and organizing your space not only lets you know about the stuff that you have, but it can also save you a lot of time, since you will know where to find something when you need it. Now, when you wake up early in the morning, you don't have to search frantically as minutes tick by for your special pair of shoes, your watch, or the blouse that you really wanted to wear. The start of your day will be a smooth one instead, and you will be able to make it out of the door to your work or college on time.

4. You will be more social

Would you like your friend to see your messy room? I would probably be too embarrassed if my friend came over and got to look at my room in a messy state. When you are ashamed of the state of your bedroom, it is less likelihood that you invite anyone over. On the other hand, when your house is clean, you are ready for company and are also more likely to invite or welcome someone over on the spur of the moment. Tidying your room helps in preventing the creation of a boundary around you; therefore, you will become more social.

5. Your health will improve

Tidying your room also bring with itself some health benefits. When your bedroom becomes a peaceful and ordered place with no clutter around, you will feel less stressed and less distracted. This means you can spend some relaxing time before bed and go to sleep calmly. From studies, it has been found that those who have cluttered bedrooms full of their hoardings take a long time to fall asleep and their sleep quality is also poor enough that it leads an increase chance of depression and stress. It's clear enough. Tidying your room will have a positive effect on your health and the thought of going to the bedroom would be a pleasant and calming one. Not just this, but a tidy room will no more be home to bacteria and viruses that can compromise your health.

13. Waiting in for a delivery

When we purchase a product online, our mind experiences a sense of virtual ownership, and the endowment effect kicks in

Not too long ago, I decided to replace my old smartphone. As I placed the order for a new one from a Seattle based e-commerce company, I felt a strange sense of uneasiness and impatience. I decided to do what any scientifically curious person in a predicament would.

I googled it.

There it was on Urban Dictionary, a crowdsourced online dictionary for slang words and phrases: “Pre-Parcel Anxiety".

“The nervous impatience experienced when waiting for a parcel or package you’ve ordered to be delivered. Often accompanied by frequent glances at the front door for signs of the courier driver when you hear any audible or visual queues of their presence."

But why does this benign vagary of the mind occur? Digging deep into behavioural economics, I discovered that the endowment effect could help us make sense of it.

A term coined by Nobel laureate Richard Thaler, the endowment effect is a cognitive bias that transpires when individuals value something that they already own more than something that they do not yet own. Once we purchase a product, we start to experience an innate sense of ownership, end up giving more value to it and start envisioning all the ways in which it would give us joy or improve our lives.

While shopping at brick-and-mortar stores, the time gap between the actual purchase and the use of the product is negligible. On the other hand, when we purchase a product online, our mind experiences a sense of virtual ownership, and the endowment effect kicks in. This tension between experiencing a heightened sense of entitlement for a product and a delay of a few days in physical ownership makes our mind act in a manner that seems irrational.

Owning a specific brand helps consumers express and build their own self-image. Management psychologist M. Joseph Sirgy’s self-congruity theory suggests that consumer behaviour is partially determined by the similarity between the consumers’ self-image and their perception of the brand’s image. Positive self-congruity, the scenario where brand image and the self-image resemble each other, enhances the endowment effect. This is especially lucrative for online retailers who, by mining user data, are able to send unique targeted advertisements to each potential buyer to achieve greater positive self-congruity than their brick-and-mortar counterparts.

Tracking the whereabouts of the order through the online merchant's website doesn't help neutralize pre-parcel anxiety. Au contraire, by giving us more information about the package, it gives impetus to the endowment effect.

The uneasiness after placing the order was also coupled with a high level of excitement. As the delivery man rang the doorbell, the euphoria had reached untenable levels. I unboxed my phone, admired its stunning partial glass back that a certain Mountain View, California-based company had done an exemplary job with.

But there was still an unanswered question. I was more than satisfied with my purchase, but the excitement had subdued. Shouldn't the joy of physically possessing something be greater than the joy of merely anticipating its arrival?

It didn't make sense to me, till I explored another branch of social science: evolutionary psychology.

By virtue of natural selection, we are programmed to perform certain acts such as having sex or eating, acts that take our genes forward to subsequent generations. Hence, pleasure is just an evolutionary tool to get us to make an effort to execute these acts. But pleasure can't last forever because if it doesn't recede, we wouldn't go after it again. For instance, our body needs to chase the pleasure of eating every day, or it wouldn't get its dose of food for survival. Biologically, pleasure needs to be fleeting and leave us repeatedly underwhelmed after we've achieved it. Thus, the pleasure derived from the anticipation of an event (using a new phone in my case) is always greater than the pleasure derived from the event itself.

In a study by Read Montague, a neuroscientist, it was shown that the mere sight of a Coke label was sufficient to activate the brain's pleasure centres by elevating the levels of dopamine, a neurotransmitter that helps control the brain's reward and pleasure centres. According to Robert Wright, an evolutionary psychologist, this pre-sip elevation of dopamine is always much greater than the post-sip spike. Wright explains: "The drop in dopamine is, in a way, the breaking of the promise—or, at least, it's a kind of biochemical acknowledgement that there was some overpromising. To the extent that you bought the promise—anticipated greater pleasure than would be delivered by the consumption itself—you have been, if not deluded, at least misled."

So behavioural economics cleared my doubts about pre-parcel anxiety and natural selection perfectly explained my varying levels of excitement over the process of purchasing a phone, but is there any merit in being aware of our cognitive biases and illusions?

Perhaps. Perhaps not.

I believe what Yongey Mingyur Rinpoche, a Tibetan Buddhist guru, says about mental afflictions is true for all kinds of human behavioural aberrations. That at the end of the day it boils down to choosing between the discomfort of becoming aware of them or the discomfort of being ruled by them.

10 Fun and Productive Ways to Pass Your Time While Waiting for a Package

The faster the tempo of our lives is, the more unbearable waiting becomes. Is a friend late for three minutes? Is your flight delayed by half an hour? Is a package delivery late? Some of us are getting so anxious in these situations — one would easily set the world on fire. However, long waiting times and shipment delays are inevitable in this world. Especially now, when the postal system is affected by the COVID crisis, political struggles, and other critical developments. Unfortunately, delivery problems have affected BooksRun as well — how frustrating and tedious are those extended waiting times for a textbook you need so much... However, waiting for a package might not be such an annoying thing. Here we've picked 10 productive and fun activities you can enjoy while your textbooks are on their way to you!

Want to know a fun fact about delivery waiting? Even if a shipment is not delayed, you're still anxious about receiving it — you want to grasp that ordered thing right now. The Urban Dictionary even suggests a name for this phenomenon — "pre-parcel anxiety". This state of waiting for a parcel is "often accompanied by frequent glances at the front door for signs of the courier driver when you hear any audible or visual queues of their presence." Does it sound familiar?

We experience this anxiety for a reason: let's say in a bookstore, you enjoy your purchase the very moment you paid for it. You immediately get a brand new textbook or a guide for your next journey destination you've given tones of money for. However, suppose you're smart, and you use BooksRun to get cheaper textbooks. In that case, you won't get an item as soon as you pay for it — you'd need to wait several days while our partner delivery services ship it to your doorstep. But your brain treats the purchased object as your possession and sends you threatening signals: "That textbook is yours, you've bought it, why can't you use it? What delivery? You mean, someone else is having your textbook right now? Check your delivery status one more time! They've probably lost your book."

And these signals become even more disturbing if the delivery time is extended. We apologize for the inconvenience that delayed shippings can cause you. Unfortunately, we can't affect the processing times of postal services. At the same time, BooksRun believes that getting anxious about it is a very destructive behavior. Instead of updating the delivery status every five minutes or checking for the courier to appear on the corner, you can call a relative or a friend you haven't spoken to for a while. Instead of asking all your friends who also rent or buy used textbooks from BooksRun if they have already gotten their books, you can check other learning opportunities for the same subject.

I bet these activities will be a much better use of your time than all those anxiety-driven things you often turn to. So check the list below for other tips on handling your time while waiting for a package — you'll find ten excellent ideas for being productive or having fun!

Laugh

Make a meme about long waiting times and share it with your friends. Laughter is one of the best cures for hardships and boredom. Use the meme generator!

Learn

Watch YouTube videos on the subject of the textbooks you've ordered. There are some fascinating channels about science, history, and so much more.

Plan ahead

Set up your bullet journal and the schedule in the meantime. The beginning of the academic year is the best time to review your goals, clarify your daily routines, and form new habits.

Amplify

Get your hands on some new amazing apps designed to enhance your productivity at college. Notion is the new hit of this year — we've described this app and other tools in this article.

Explore

Why not start checking possible and career tracks? You can review trending college specializations, contact your college's career services, and connect to alumnae to learn more about their experiences. Even if the epidemic situation won't get better, you can still opt for a remote internship.

Wait in style

Find a book or a movie about waiting. Yes, "Hachi: A Dog's Tale" is an easy and very sentimental pick, but can you find something more creative?

Read

Catch up on some classic literature — from Plato to Harper Lee. The time you spend reading is never wasted!

Cook

Prepare something extraordinary or try a recipe you've always found fascinating. For example, you cook something that your!

Declutter

Review your clothing items, stationery, reading lists, random files on your laptop, and books — here we've described the step-by-step process of decluttering for students. Maybe there're still textbooks from previous terms you haven't sold yet? It's now or never, sell used textbooks and earn some money while waiting for your package to come!

Be grateful

Write a lifetime gratitude list. It is one of the best calming exercises that ever existed. Calmly, write down as many individuals and things you're grateful for and answer to yourself — why? Creating this list will teach you how much you already have, and your life is pretty much perfect without that thing you're waiting for. Save it for the future because reading through it from time to time (and adding new lines to it) can be an excellent resource for rooting down and feeling grateful.

Have you found something for yourself? We hope some of these activities will let your mind wander in a different direction and enhance your life quality. However, there might be a situation when your textbook is dramatically delayed, and you can't complete an assignment or prepare for an assessment test. Here we've reviewed the reasons behind these shortcomings. We also want to give you some troubleshooting tips to handle this situation successfully. First, you can ask your friends to share the materials or to work on some assignments together. Then, you can also talk to your professor. If you didn't get the book on time, but you need to do an assignment based on it — try to explain to your instructor why this delay occurred (because it's not your fault) and ask for a possible solution. Maybe they can propose you a different assignment or move the deadline for a later date. In any case, don't underestimate how understanding people can be!

14. The Kardashians

The Kardashian extended family has been a reality TV staple since Keeping Up with the Kardashians premiered in 2007. It was one of the first reality shows and shaped a whole new genre of television. The final season premiered early this spring, in March 2021.

It has run for 20 seasons and revolves around the lives of the Kardashian sisters: Kim, Kourtney, and Khloe. Half-sisters Kendall and Kylie Jenner are also featured, as well as Kris Jenner and Caitlyn Jenner. Keeping Up with the Kardashians is the very definition of a guilty pleasure, but recently, some fans have been critical.

The Kardashian extended family has been a reality TV staple since Keeping Up with the Kardashians premiered in 2007. It was one of the first reality shows and shaped a whole new genre of television. The final season premiered early this spring, in March 2021.

(L-R) Khloe Kardashian, Kendall Jenner, Kim Kardashian, Kourtney Kardashian and Kris Jenner | Todd Williamson/Getty Images

It has run for 20 seasons and revolves around the lives of the Kardashian sisters: Kim, Kourtney, and Khloe. Half-sisters Kendall and Kylie Jenner are also featured, as well as Kris Jenner and Caitlyn Jenner. Keeping Up with the Kardashians is the very definition of a guilty pleasure, but recently, some fans have been critical.

Keeping Up With the Kardashians rocketed the family into fame

The Kardashians have faced criticisms since their first episode debuted. Critics have panned the series almost from the moment it aired. The concept of being famous for simply being famous lacked intelligence, critics say. Fans love their guilty pleasures, though.

Ryan Seacrest developed the show, with Kris Jenner fully on board. Following the lives of the Kardashian-Jenner clan seemed to be the perfect recipe for drama. They were described as crazy and fun-loving together, and the series was bankrolled. Kim Kardashian was one of the biggest reasons why the show was greenlit.

Kim worked as a celebrity stylist and had a job with Paris Hilton. She was often featured on Hilton's reality show, The Simple Life. She was in the public eye as a personal friend of Hilton's and eventually started working with other celebrities, such as Lindsay Lohan. It was her sextape, though, that launched her into fame, and helped get Keeping Up With the Kardashians on the air.

Fans share opinions on why the show has become boring

Keeping Up With the Kardashians is somewhat formulaic. The show opens by showing off the wealthy lifestyle of the Kardashian-Jenner clan, then moves into family troubles that are quickly resolved. Most episodes end with a monologue about the importance of family. Fans loved the drama. Lately, though, some fans have found the show getting boring.

The Kardashian extended family has been a reality TV staple since Keeping Up with the Kardashians premiered in 2007. It was one of the first reality shows and shaped a whole new genre of television. The final season premiered early this spring, in March 2021.

(L-R) Khloe Kardashian, Kendall Jenner, Kim Kardashian, Kourtney Kardashian and Kris Jenner | Todd Williamson/Getty Images

It has run for 20 seasons and revolves around the lives of the Kardashian sisters: Kim, Kourtney, and Khloe. Half-sisters Kendall and Kylie Jenner are also featured, as well as Kris Jenner and Caitlyn Jenner. Keeping Up with the Kardashians is the very definition of a guilty pleasure, but recently, some fans have been critical.

Keeping Up With the Kardashians rocketed the family into fame

The Kardashians have faced criticisms since their first episode debuted. Critics have panned the series almost from the moment it aired. The concept of being famous for simply being famous lacked intelligence, critics say. Fans love their guilty pleasures, though.

Ryan Seacrest developed the show, with Kris Jenner fully on board. Following the lives of the Kardashian-Jenner clan seemed to be the perfect recipe for drama. They were described as crazy and fun-loving together, and the series was bankrolled. Kim Kardashian was one of the biggest reasons why the show was greenlit.

Kim worked as a celebrity stylist and had a job with Paris Hilton. She was often featured on Hilton's reality show, The Simple Life. She was in the public eye as a personal friend of Hilton's and eventually started working with other celebrities, such as Lindsay Lohan. It was her sextape, though, that launched her into fame, and helped get Keeping Up With the Kardashians on the air.

Fans share opinions on why the show has become boring

Keeping Up With the Kardashians is somewhat formulaic. The show opens by showing off the wealthy lifestyle of the Kardashian-Jenner clan, then moves into family troubles that are quickly resolved. Most episodes end with a monologue about the importance of family. Fans loved the drama. Lately, though, some fans have found the show getting boring.

While formulaic in the earlier seasons, there was always drama. Whether it was Kim's highly public divorce with Kris Humphries, or family fights, fans always had something to talk about. This last season, though, has fans talking for entirely different reasons.

There's no drama anymore, according to fans on Reddit. Kim used to play with her kids, for example, but fans think that the need to keep a specific public image has kept them from showing more of their personalities. The Kardashian-Jenner girls have built careers and businesses based on their particular fashion and style.

Kim Kardashian West has built KKW, a beauty brand, and Skims, a shapewear brand. She was on Time's 2015 list of 10 most influential people, thanks to her companies, her political lobbying, and Keeping Up With the Kardashians. Kylie Jenner has founded the beauty company Kylie, and sister Kendall is a model.

They depend almost solely on their reputation and appearance to stay famous, and fans think that may be why the series has gotten boring. They don't feel like they have the freedom to be themselves like they were in earlier seasons. With brands that revolve around a specific look, fans think that the show has become more a commercial for their respective brands rather than a look into their lives.

With fashion and beauty being their main business, they have to look perfect every episode. Fans want something more personal.

15. People who Instagram their food

Originally launched in 2010, Instagram was created for photo and video sharing, allowing its users to present a curated (and distorted) version of their lives. Essentially, it was born as the next big social media after Facebook had begun its decline, as Instagram managed to succeed in ways the Blue App couldn't (and more). With its sleek and minimalistic design, and the fun and beautifying filters, the new platform was able to capture the younger generation, and thus take over the world. From the rise of the so-called "Instagram models" and other influencers, the app has been able to leave a mark on the current cultural and societal landscape. It has helped shape our beauty standards, for better or for worse (especially for worse), as well as connecting people from all around the globe. It's more than just an app – it's a cultural powerhouse. Unfortunately, after eleven years since its first appearance in our App Stores, Instagram is slowly dying... actually, it might already be dead.

I don't know about you, but I still remember when I first opened the Instagram app. It was eight years ago, I was sitting on my bedroom floor with a friend and in a moment of youthful bravado, we had decided to forgo our parents' "no social media" rule and download the thrilling popular app. It's been almost a decade and a lot has changed – for me and for Instagram. Though, one of us has changed for the worst, and it's safe to say it is not me. All great empires fall at some point, and rumor has it that Instagram's decline already has begun.

Instagram is dying' – what does that mean?

Many people hear this phrase and think it means that Instagram as a company or product is failing miserably, and is one inconvenience away from going belly up. Let's get one thing straight – that is NOT what it means. The platform is definitely still growing, it still has tons of active users (over 1B), and it is still making a shitload of money – in a nutshell, Instagram is doing just fine on the surface. But even though numbers don't lie, neither do I.

Instagram may still be experiencing growth in the number of its active users – however, it's been a very slow growth since 2019, and has even dropped to single digits. I may not know much about the stock market, but even I understand that "slow growth" for a company that once held the world in a tight grip, is a codeword for "losing money". Since the platform's future is not looking exactly rosy, investors are beginning to look elsewhere, and leaving Instagram behind to go down on its own.

But why is that?

Originally launched in 2010, Instagram was created for photo and video sharing, allowing its users to present a curated (and distorted) version of their lives. Essentially, it was born as the next big social media after Facebook had begun its decline, as Instagram managed to succeed in ways the Blue App couldn't (and more). With its sleek and minimalistic design, and the fun and beautifying filters, the new platform was able to capture the younger generation, and thus take over the world. From the rise of the so-called "Instagram models" and other influencers, the app has been able to leave a mark on the current cultural and societal landscape. It has helped shape our beauty standards, for better or for worse (especially for worse), as well as connecting people from all around the globe. It's more than just an app – it's a cultural powerhouse. Unfortunately, after eleven years since its first appearance in our App Stores, Instagram is slowly dying... actually, it might already be dead.

I don't know about you, but I still remember when I first opened the Instagram app. It was eight years ago, I was sitting on my bedroom floor with a friend and in a moment of youthful bravado, we had decided to forgo our parents' "no social media" rule and download the thrilling popular app. It's been almost a decade and a lot has changed – for me and for Instagram. Though, one of us has changed for the worst, and it's safe to say it is not me. All great empires fall at some point, and rumor has it that Instagram's decline already has begun.

'Instagram is dying' – what does that mean?

Many people hear this phrase and think it means that Instagram as a company or product is failing miserably, and is one inconvenience away from going belly up. Let's get one thing straight – that is NOT what it means. The platform is definitely still growing, it still has tons of active users (over 1B), and it is still making a shitload of money – in a nutshell, Instagram is doing just fine on the surface. But even though numbers don't lie, neither do I.

Instagram may still be experiencing growth in the number of its active users – however, it's been a very slow growth since 2019, and has even dropped to single digits. I may not know much about the stock market, but even I understand that "slow growth" for a company that once held the world in a tight grip, is a codeword for "losing money". Since the platform's future is not looking exactly rosy, investors are beginning to look elsewhere, and leaving Instagram behind to go down on its own.

But why is that?

The algorithm is making things hard for... everyone

For starters, Instagram's algorithm has been pissing off a lot of people for a while – both the Average Joes of Instagram, and its Influencers.

If you are part of the first category, the algorithm screws you over as it makes your experience on the app messy and disorganized. Thanks to a recent update, the posts you see on your timeline are not in chronological order (!), but you only see posts based on how popular they are. Thus, you don't even get to see everything uploaded by the people you follow. Then,

Instagram's explore page is extremely lackluster, and is more often than not filled with TikTok's reuploads and knockoffs.

But as Instagram is now prioritizing popular uploads, and due to the lack of a reshare feature, smaller creators find themselves at a disadvantage.

From an Instagram Influencer's perspective, this algorithm is even more maddening. Since only the most popular posts are boosted, smaller creators are having a tougher time reaching new audiences, building a following and promoting their own posts. It's incredibly frustrating, since plenty of people rely on Instagram and advertising through the platform as their source of revenue, and they are now seeing their levels of engagement drop dramatically.

Instagram's whole appeal for influencers was that it made it possible for anyone to get popular and go viral on the network. If people liked your posts, it didn't matter if you were a celebrity, or had 10M followers or just a few hundreds – anyone could have a shot at becoming an influencer. But as Instagram is now prioritizing popular uploads, and due to the lack of a reshare feature, smaller creators find themselves at a disadvantage. Hence, more and more people are growing annoyed and frustrated with the social network, and are attempting to find solace in the arms of other platforms (namely, TikTok and Twitter).

Instagram's core purpose has always been about sharing photos and videos, and that proved to be a successful business idea since the app's very beginning. However, quickly after the platform's launch, a new competitor came along, and gave Instagram a run for its money – Snapchat.

If you're not familiar with this social media (and let's be fair – who isn't), its main concept is snapping photos and videos, which vanish after 24 hours. (Un)surprisingly, the platform received massive success, as users really seemed to dig the whole "disappearing posts" idea. In an attempt to remain ahead of the game, Instagram tried to buy Snapchat, but their offer was rejected. So, they decided to just copy the competition, and out popped "Instagram Stories" (i.e., the exact same thing as Snapchat). Their plan worked wonders, as Instagram managed to trump superior after the introduction of Stories, and was once again back at the top of the social media podium. But here's where things went sideways.

Instagram tried to do too much too fast, prioritizing speed of product delivery over quality, and weakened themselves while trying to diversify their content.

Seeing how well their escamotage worked, Instagram started copying... everyone. YouTube became IGTV, Facebook Marketplace became Instagram Marketplace, the Twitter Explore Page became the Instagram Explore Page, and TikTok became Reels. Unfortunately, the strategy didn't quite work out this time around.

Trying to keep up with the competition, Instagram became too cluttered, and lost its simple raison d'être – sharing pictures. Plus, all the copies are merely bootleg versions of the original features – they're messy, not well-organized, and constitute an afterthought for most people, as they use Instagram merely to repost content they have already uploaded on other media. Users still prefer YouTube and TikTok over IGTV and Reels, and... well, nobody uses Instagram Marketplace.

Instagram tried to do too much too fast, prioritizing speed of product delivery over quality, and weakened themselves while trying to diversify their content. They lost sight of their own strengths, and entered the path to failure all by themselves.

A major obstacle Instagram has had to face in recent times has been capturing the attention of those under 18, aka Generation Z and Generation Alpha. Despite once being the no. 1 app amongst young audiences, users aged 13-17 on the platform now reach a mere 3.7%.

Why? Well, first of all Gen Z/Alpha is known to be a more skeptical generation in regards to social media – they crave anonymity, safety from online bullying and hate speech, and definitely hate ads. Ergo, why would they choose a platform that is known to spy on its users, and is a playground for advertisers?

On top of that, most people would agree that Instagram has become quite boring. It doesn't offer the witty jokes or interesting threads you can find on Twitter, nor the fun or useful videos you can stumble upon on TikTok. All it has are overly-curated feeds of influencers that just do not fit in with the young generation, who is more geared towards spontaneity and playful candidness.

Plus, as Instagram is still going strong among older generations (Millennials and Baby Boomers), more and more young people are steering away from it. After all, no one wants to be on the same social network as their mom or their uncle! That's the same thing that happened to Facebook, which – albeit managing to keep it financially afloat – has been more detrimental than good, as it has made it fade into irrelevance.

16. Football pundits' analysis

People can make some rather vacuous remarks, and for real bona fide stupidity, look no further than football punditry.

BT Sport's Michael Owen, for example, may have been a formidable striker, but his monotone, headache inducing 'insights' leave a lot to be desired. Ridiculed since his punditry debut a couple of years ago, relying heavily on footballing clichés and unemotional observations, Mike-otron 2000 is the commentary equivalent of a vegan doughnut: bland and boring

Football Punditry: The Good, The Bland and The Boring

Owen has spouted some inane observations, however, the following six statements really highlight his punditry prowess:

1. "It's a good run but it's a poor run, if you know what I mean?" (We don't, please elaborate)

2. "What a feeling it is to be a manager and bring someone on."

3. "It's a nightmare for strikers when defences push up. You've got to go with them or you're offside." (Thanks for clarifying, Michael)

4. "That's simple as...simple"

6. You have to believe your own eyes, don't you?"

6. "To stay in the game, you have to stay in the game". (Straight out of Sun Tzu's "The Art of War)

Please, Michael, think before you talk, you're making my migraine twerk. Then there's Robbie Savage. While he is an improvement on Owen, that doesn't say much for the ex footballer. When Manchester United legend Paul Scholes was caught muttering an obscenity in the direction of Savage on BT Sport's Fletch & Sav show, he was speaking for the vast majority of football fans.

Scholes muttered 'k***head' under his breath, and this assertion, more accurate than any football based one ever made by Savage, hit the nail firmly on the head. By bellowing a mishmash of guess-timations, Savage seems reliant upon two 'go to' words when describing a particular piece of footage: Incredible and Disgraceful.

Possibly his most insightful moment arrived after England were prematurely eliminated from last year's World Cup. When asked where it all went wrong for Roy's men, Savage stated that England's simply failed to "have a go." Perhaps Roy Hodgson, after hearing this, thought "damn it, that Savage has a point. If only we had a go."

Every family has a black sheep. Just ask Bill Clinton. If you weren't aware that the ex, fun-loving president had a brother, it's for one simple reason: Bill wanted it that way. While 'Wild Bill' was seducing interns and becoming a prominent world leader, his half-brother Roger was involved in cocaine trafficking.

How Gary Neville must feel when his brother Phil decides to open his mouth, probably the same way Bill feels when Roger comes to town. Inferior in every way imaginable, Phil never was the footballer Gary was. Although he was a very respectable defender/holding midfielder, Phil's punditry leaves a lot to be desired. In fact, no sooner had he made his co-commentary debut alongside Guy Mowbray for England vs Italy, close to 500 people called the BBC to complain.

Mercilessly ridiculed on Twitter for his debut nose dive, Pip responded in a manner that showed genuine good spirit, taking to Twitter to apologise in a humble, slightly embarrassing manner.

At the other end of the sibling spectrum sits Gary Neville, a man widely regarded as the best analyst currently operating today. The former Manchester United and England defender, once the UK's least popular player, is now a beloved pundit.

What makes Gary Neville such a celebrated pundit? Firstly, as obvious as it sounds, he actually fills the job description. No sitting on the fence here, Neville refuses to remain 'Swiss'. His step-by-step, analytical approach is masterful, a joy to behold. Making it look effortless, that is where his genius lies.

One would assume that shedding light upon a sport you've played at an elite level shouldn't be particularly difficult, however, Michael Owen shows that this is a flawed philosophy. Thirteen years ago, whilst sidelined with a broken metatarsal, Neville made his punditry debut for ITV at the 2002 World Cup.

Regularly seated beside the likes of Jamie Redknapp and Thierry Henry, two very uncontroversial gentlemen, you could be forgiven for thinking Neville's quality is amplified by some of the other Sky Sports pundits.

Although, on closer analysis, one sees just how good Neville really is.

In stark contrast to most of the flock, he argues against the consensus. Also, just because Neville was one of Manchester United's longest serving players, bias never plays a part in his analysis.

For example, back in January, Neville criticized Louis van Gaal's 3-5-2 system, saying it had made Manchester United too slow and predictable.

United supporters were obviously siding with the pundit, regularly shouting '4-4-2' at home and away fixtures.

Analysing United on Monday Night Football, Sky Sports' stellar show, Neville said Van Gaal's 3-5-2 system lacked dynamism and merely favoured possession over attacking play.

Honestly and precisely, the class of 92 graduate said: "They play the ball out from the back – as most good teams would – but the tempo is too slow."

Furthermore, prior to this observation, when United sold Danny Welbeck to Arsenal, Neville told Talksport, "I can't work it out, after all the prices I've seen paid this summer, I'm thinking 'how is it just £16million? There's been right-backs and left-backs galore who have been bought for £15million this summer. How have they got him for £16million? I can't work it out to this day, it's a strange one. It really does feel strange that it's a centre forward and actually it's helped out a competitor, someone who will be vying for those third and four places with United this season."

Jamie Redknapp, on the other hand, remains totally neutral, determined not to be overly critical. Considering he appears to be friendly with, or related to, a number of leading Premier League figures, how is Redknapp supposed to provide the viewer with meaningful, honest thoughts? Successfully avoiding such partisanship, Neville isn't afraid to tell it like it is, even if he currently holds a key coaching role with the English national team.

Neville's Monday Night Football musings, a show where he demonstrates his real skill, are obviously the result of diligent, methodical research. When the two time Champions League winner put a 16-minute sequence on the art of diving together at the end of last season, many people took to Twitter to praise his endeavour and insight. You see, Neville was a true pro, a footballer all too aware of his strengths and weaknesses. Now, undeniably, the 40 year old treats punditry in very much the same way he treated his playing career. He wasn't the fastest, he wasn't the most skilful, he wasn't the most naturally gifted, but Neville succeeded through blood, sweat and meticulous preparation.

17. Unnecessary meetings

3 Ways to Eliminate Unnecessary Meetings

Unproductive business meetings not only waste time, they are also costly for a company.

Meetings are a necessary evil in business life. They are essential to reach agreements with the different parts of a company, but if they are not carried out correctly they can cause great losses of time .

There are times when the description of the objective of the meeting is confusing, there is no agenda, minutes of a previous meeting to follow up on the decisions reached - if there were any - and half of the people called do not know why they are there.

These meetings quickly "break down" to see various issues that lead nowhere or to resolve issues that have not been able to vent in other forums. There is no shortage of the assistant who decides to take advantage of his time with his smartphone , while others chat with each other.

These are the least productive meetings in the world.

According to Industry Week , 15 percent of total work time is wasted in meetings and that percentage rises to 40 percent when it comes to senior executives. This translates to two days a week dedicated only to meeting with three or more coworkers.

What's more, in the United States alone, these unnecessary meetings result in losses of $ 37 billion in salary costs.

1. Think it over before inviting everyone

Before organizing a meeting ask yourself: Is it essential to have a meeting? Maybe you can solve the pending issues with a couple of calls.

You should also think about who are the people who must necessarily attend the meeting because their presence is vital to address the problem in question.

2. Establish a reason

It is essential that you indicate why the participants should attend the meeting and what you hope to achieve. Don't forget to offer attendees the option of not attending if they believe their presence cannot contribute in a meaningful way to the purpose of the meeting.

3. Be thorough with the details

The joints must be correct:

-Keep a clear agenda for the meeting.

-If necessary, send reading materials in advance.

-Set a start time and a maximum end time for the meeting.

-Avoid falling into points not established in the agenda.

-Raise a minute of the agreed points.

Like many of you, I spend a lot of time in meetings in my job. Sometimes I am the leader/organizer of the meeting, and many times I am an invitee. Either way, I feel slightly qualified, simply based on experience, to provide some insight to help you determine if the meeting you are leading or participating in is ineffective or not. If your organization is like most others, you probably have weekly department meetings, weekly management meetings or regular Sr. Leadership meetings. The point being, you invest somewhere between 2-4 hours of your work week into these types of meetings each and every week. You want to make sure that the time spent is valuable. Far too many companies get focused on the routine and simply have meetings for the sake of having meetings. As you can imagine (and have lived it) this is a colossal time and money suck.

Before you can determine if your meetings are effective or not, you need to know the signs of ineffective meetings as these are quite overt and should be the first indication you may be in for a waste of time if you attend. Think of them more as red flags; that is, if you see more than two of these signs, odds are your meeting is going to be ineffective – whether you are leading it or are participating in it.

Signs of ineffective meetings:

1. No agenda – this is the biggest red flag of all. If there is no agenda, or simply a meeting request, or worse yet, a recycled agenda (i.e. same one used week over week with slight modifications) you are in for an ineffective meeting.

2. No clear meeting organizer – a meeting is called, but there is a lack of clarity around who is organizing it and for what purpose. The meeting request may have been sent out by someone's admin. assistant but there is no clear subject or purpose indicated for the meeting request. This typically feeds into point #1 above as you can be sure there is not going to be an agenda either.

3. No minutes are taken at the meeting – without minutes, details are lost, action items are missed and there are no clear takeaway's for anyone. This results in gaps, lack of accountability and frustration for all.

4. The meeting doesn't start/end on time – this is a clear sign, especially when it occurs on a semi-regular basis, that the meeting isn't a priority for the organizer and/or the attendees aren't accountable for arriving on time. It shows a lack of respect for the attendees and it also sends the message that the meeting really isn't that much of a priority because whatever was

happening before hand was way more important.

5. Communication is one way – you often see this when someone "in charge" calls a meeting and it simply is that person "pushing" information to the others in attendance. There is no opportunity for questions, comments, exchange of ideas, etc.

6. The meeting organizer controls communication – this occurs when the organizer (often a department head) calls for meetings and uses them as a way to check in with his/her staff. Instead of having regular 1:1's with them, he/she gets their staff together, calls it a meeting, and then runs through a series of updates/exchanges with the members of their team. It looks/feels like this: Dept. head asks Manager A for an update, Manager A provides this update. Dept. head asks Manager B for an update, Manager B provides the update and around we go. There is no discussion or dialogue amongst the peer group, no exchange of ideas or best practices. The meeting is simply used by the department manager as a way to check in with his/her staff, while wasting everyone else's time as they do so.

7. There is no participation by the attendees– during the meeting, the participants have no information to share, they are not prepared, and they have no updates, no ideas or thoughts to contribute. An opportunity to learn and share best practices from amongst a peer group has been lost. If this is the case, you either have an ineffective meeting leader (because they should not allow participants to do this) or you have the wrong people invited to your meeting. Either way, these are both signs of an ineffective meeting.

8. There is no clear "act" that comes from the meeting – when getting a group of managers together for meetings, there should be a clear "act" required and a follow up for the next meeting. The act may be a request to communicate something to staff, to provide feedback on a process, or to deliver a budget update. Either way, meeting participants leave the meeting with a clear understanding of what they need to do or "act" upon. An ineffective meeting has occurred when participants leave the meeting saying things like: "What was the purpose of that meeting?" or "What exactly am I supposed to do now?" or "Why did they need us there, couldn't they have just send us an email?"

Meetings are a necessary evil, but sometimes, they seem less necessary and more evil than they have to be.

"Meetings should be like salt—a spice sprinkled carefully to enhance a dish," says Basecamp founder and CEO, Jason Fried. "Too much salt destroys a dish. Too many meetings destroy morale and motivation."

That's because excessive meetings tend to be draining on employees and waste company time.

A Clarizen/Harris Poll survey reveals that the average American worker spends 4.5 hours in general status meetings each week, and workers spend even longer (4.6 hours) just preparing for those meetings. Almost half of the survey respondents stated that they would rather perform some type of unpleasant activity—including visits to the dentist or nightmarishly-long commutes—than attend a status meeting.

CEOs spend the equivalent of two work days each week in meetings, according to a study by Bain & Company. At one organisation, Bain found that attendees spent 7,000 hours a year in the weekly senior leadership meeting, and subordinates spent 300,000 hours in related meetings and prep time!

So, how can executives stop wasting their time—and everyone else's—in meetings?

Most companies do a thorough job of conducting cost analyses before embarking on projects or hiring employees, but they rarely evaluate the cost of a meeting.

"Meetings can be a waste of time and money, and anytime a meeting is going on, those who are in the meeting should be aware of how much that meeting is costing the company and evaluating whether or not it is worth it," according to Bonnie Hagemann, co-author of "Leading with Vision" and CEO of Executive Development Associates.

"Just look around your next meeting, estimate the salary of those in the room, turn it into hourly and then add up how much that meeting is costing the company," she suggests.

Hagemann says she once worked with a company that held an executive meeting every Friday. She crunched the numbers and discovered that it cost the company $10,000 a week for that meeting. The company accordingly made changes to their meetings, including cutting the frequency down to just two times a month.

Consider trimming the fat off of your meetings' length.

While meetings are typically blocked on the hour, Hagemann recommends ending them as soon as the work is complete.

"Don't linger and talk about other unproductive topics just because you have an hour blocked on your calendar," Hagemann says.

In fact, she's in favor of scheduling meetings for 30 minutes.

"If you need more time, you'll find it," she explains. "And, whenever possible, don't call a meeting at all—sometimes a 5-minute phone call can resolve an issue."

Cameron Herold, founder of the COO Alliance, and author of "Meetings Suck," believes that face-to-face meetings are important, but stresses that leaders need to be efficient in meetings. When vital information is shared via phone or email, he warns that body language and facial cues can't be interpreted. In fact, Herold says it's impossible to know if the team is even paying attention.

Sometimes, the decision to have a meeting or not should be based on what you're trying to accomplish. Michael Fritsch, GM of Consulting for Confoe, a project management consulting firm in Austin, TX, recommends specific meeting types depending on your objectives:

1. Problem solving meeting:

use to work through an issue or solve a problem

limit attendance to important stakeholders and those who can solve the issue

2. Decision-making meeting:

may be a presentation of options to the decision maker

use when the facts have been investigated and you are ready to move forward

3. Planning meeting:

use to plan a course of action

like the problem-solving meeting, limit attendance to important stakeholders and those who will execute the planned work

4. Status reporting/information sharing meeting:

easiest type of meeting to eliminate

objectives can usually be more efficiently accomplished by a written report, dashboard, on-demand webcast or e-mail newsletter

no need for an actual meeting unless there are likely to be a lot of questions or you need interaction for political or motivational purposes (for example, reporting quarterly results and thanking the department may be better in a meeting than a memo)

5. Feedback meeting:

use to ask participants to react to recent events or information, or to evaluate proposals

objective may be met by other means (i.e. sending an e-mail, posting information to a web site, sending a survey, or using reports, dashboards, and other electronic status updates)

limit attendance to relevant players

Have an agenda and clear objectives to run an efficient meeting.

“Only meet when there has been an agenda published prior to the meeting,” Fritsch says. “If you are invited to a meeting that doesn’t have an agenda, decline the meeting—although this may be difficult if [the host] is your boss.”

“Objectives should be clear and materials necessary to making a decision should be distributed in advance,” according to Heidi Pozzo, founder of Pozzo Consulting. In fact, Pozzo says attendees should know what decisions they’ll be making in the meeting, and should be prepared to discuss any issues or ask questions.

“You don’t need to cover items that are on track, just the items that need course corrections,” Pozzo says. “If you focus on these topics, you will eliminate a lot of non-value added discussion.”

She also recommends starting meetings on time. “Many companies waste 5-10 minutes of each meeting waiting for people to get there and catching people up who were late,” Pozzo says. “Start the meeting on time and don’t catch people up; they will learn to be on time quickly.”

Empower others to lead meetings for added efficiency.

Consider training your employees to run a meeting without you. According to Herold, the average cost of training an employee to run a meeting is just £11 (around $15). Compare that to what it costs an organisation to have you present every time.

Passing the meeting baton is not only a time- and cost-effective move, it can also help to engage your employees. But, before you can train others, you may have to retrain yourself.

“Many leaders bring their selfish need to be the smartest person in the room to the meeting,” according to Dudley Slater, co-founder and former CEO of Integra Telecom, and co-author of “Fusion Leadership.”

“As Type A individuals, many of us leaders get impatient and convince ourselves that driving a meeting with our own ideas and agenda is the fastest path from starting the meeting to concluding results and directives with our team,” he says.

Slater admits that this approach is time-efficient. “However, this railroad approach to conducting meetings can leave the best ideas hidden below the surface, locked in the minds of your team, who are too intimidated or frightened to speak up,” Slater warns. “Effective leaders learn to conduct efficient meetings that foster genuine debate, probing for solutions that best serve the organisation."

18.Cleaning the bathroom

Does anyone really love to clean the bathroom? No, I didn't think so ?

When I was little, my mom used to make up games to make it more fun. "Let's see if you can get all these towels folded in two minutes. Go!" Then I'd rush to get everything done before the timer ran out.

Nowadays, no one claps and cheers when we finish folding towels or scrubbing the sink. But there's no reason we can't still make bathroom cleaning a little more enjoyable! Are you with me?

How to make bathroom cleaning fun

Make it a game

Cleaning the bathroom always feels like it takes forever, but you'd be surprised how little time tasks actually take. I like to set a timer like my mom used to do and see how quickly I can complete each task.

For example, it only takes one minute to wipe down the counters and sink — and makes a huge difference in how clean our bathroom feels. Who knew?

Buy cleaners that smell fantastic

Nice smelling cleaners go a long way toward making the bathroom cleaning experience more pleasant. I actually look forward to using this Mrs. Meyer's tub & tile cleaner — it cleans effortlessly and smells so fresh!

I'm using the lemon verbena scent right now, but I'm looking forward to trying the lavender next time around. The best part is there are no harsh fumes, so I don't have to hold my breath while I'm scrubbing the bathtub.

Squeeze in a workout

We all know there aren't enough hours in the day. So why not combine a few of tasks on your to-do list? Even though the bathroom is a small space, you can really work up a sweat.

I like to see how many steps I get while carrying towels to the laundry room and taking out the trash. Plus, I do a few squats and lunges while I'm washing the floors and tub.

Clean while you're in the shower

I love hot showers and could spend all day in there. So while I'm enjoying the water, I give the shower walls and glass a quick scrub down to keep them shiny. It makes cleaning the bathroom a lot less painful (and is a pretty productive use of water!).

I stash my Mrs. Meyer's tub & tile and Grove Collaborative scrubber sponge on the ledge in my shower as a reminder. The Grove sponges are perfect because the non-abrasive scouring side gets into the grout while the soft side gets the glass squeaky clean.

Listen to an audiobook or a podcast

Playlists are a great way to pump yourself up when you're cleaning. But lately I've discovered that listening to audiobooks while I'm cleaning is a great way to catch up on reading that I wouldn't otherwise have time for. I usually get so engrossed in my page-turner that the time flies by.

Podcasts are another fun way to make cleaning time just fly by. I've learned so much from listening to experts talk about motherhood, parenting, faith and business while doing my household chores ?

Treat yourself

Beautiful soaps, hand lotion, or a bouquet of flowers are a nice reward for all your hard work. The Mrs. Meyer's soaps and lotions are a super luxurious treat — no artificial scents here, just essential oils!

I keep my Mrs. Meyer's lemon verbena scented lotion (can you sense a pattern here?) next to the kitchen sink for easy reach. My hands are always so dry after doing the dishes!

Bonus tip: Speaking of ways to make cleaning more fun, skip the grocery store and stock up on supplies from Grove Collaborative instead. Grove delivers the best natural household products from Seventh Generation, Method, Mrs. Meyer's and more right to your door, on your schedule.

I used to hate running to the store for glass cleaner or toothpaste, but now I look forward to my monthly shipment from Grove. It feels like a present for me, but I'm actually helping my family stick to our budget! Grab your free kit and try Grove Collaborative now!

Those who have difficulty with everyday life tasks will likely have difficulty with light housekeeping and, in particular, ensuring a clean bathroom. A clean bathroom can actually affect the health and safety of aging adults and those who are housebound.

Why Is a Clean Bathroom So Important?

A clean bathroom requires wiping surfaces daily and deep cleaning weekly in order to prevent illness and infections affecting aging and/or unhealthy individuals. An unclean bathroom can affect:

Breathing – inhaling mold and dust can cause health concerns for those who may already suffer from breathing problems such as COPD, asthma, chronic bronchitis, pneumonia, or other conditions.

Microorganisms, Bacteria, Viruses, & Pathogens – can live on bathroom surfaces for up to a week or more. Keeping a clean bathroom means wiping surfaces daily with bacteria killing solutions (vinegar, bleach, antibacterial cleaners); paying special attention to the surfaces of the toilet, tub, sink and all handles & faucets. Commonly found in bathrooms:

Stomach viruses that can cause intestinal distress; viruses include E. Coli, Norovirus, and salmonella and many other bacteria and microorganisms.

Bacteria, fungi & viruses such as staph (including MRSA), athlete's feet fungus, mold & mildew (causing breathing issues to worsen or flare up), strep, and many others. Daily wiping down of your bathroom will help decrease surface bacteria/viruses/pathogens greatly.

As we age our immune systems weaken, even in those who remain active and healthy; making the probability of typical bacteria, microorganisms and viruses even more likely to affect our immune system than when we were younger.

SAFETY

It's not only important to have a clean bathroom but to make sure you provide a safe bathroom also.

Magazines & Clutter – keeping the bathroom free of clutter is part of having a clean bathroom. Having items on the floor, next to, or around the toilet area can cause falling hazards and possibly spill liquids from bottles creating slippery areas.

Throw Rugs or Bathmats – throw rugs on a floor can create a tripping hazard or sliding hazard when water gets underneath.

Tub Mats – although tub mats are created to stick to the bottom of a tub, they can often lose suction and create dangerous conditions. The mat can become bunched up and, even though the suction cups are doing their job, the mat itself can become wrinkled or turned up and cause a person to trip.

Deodorizing/Disinfectant Sprays – these sprays can create slippery surfaces if they don't dry properly and may also pose a breathing hazard for some.

Safety Bars – it is extremely important to have safety grips, bars, and pulls put in by a professional who can ensure that they are placed correctly, to handle specific weight limits safely with proper anchoring. Suction cup bars are NOT recommended and can become unattached easily.

19. Reality TV shows

Reality TV is not boring!

Reality TV is exciting and it is definitely not boring. Okay maybe the only reality TV shows I am talking about are like Masterchef Jr stuff like that but the suspense of reality TV is really outstanding and can't be beat. One thing I think though is that their lives should be more private.

20. Doing the washing-up

We've all been there: after a big meal the dishes and pots are piled up in the sink just waiting to be washed. For some, this chore is no biggie, but for others it's an onerous task that is put off until there's no more clean plates in the house. There isn't a lot of scientific research yet on why exactly so many people hate doing the dishes, but there is now a study which shows that doing the dishes is the one chore that couples fight over the most.According to a recent article in The Atlantic, doing the dishes is linked to strife among many couples. The chore is seen as disgusting and time consuming for little reward. Unlike other tasks, like say, the dinner cooked to perfection, doing the dishes offers little in the way of emotional reward from one's family. Instead the task is often taken for granted, like many of the daily tasks of cleaning up after other people. However, cleaning the bathroom or other chores aren't necessarily daily and therein lies the rub of doing the dishes.

Since 1965 the amount of housework men do in the U.S. has doubled from 2 hours a week to 4, but the number has been roughly the same since the 1990s. This means that while overall strides have been made to get men into the daily chores, the past few decades haven't yielded that much change.

Men traditionally have done the weekly tasks of yard work, taking out the garbage, and other household maintenance. But, rarely men have rarely been responsible for any major share of the cooking and cleaning up after the family.

While women's work has been steadily made easier and more efficient by modern technology – resulting in less time spent in the kitchen – women still spend on average around 14 hours a week doing housework (down from just over 30 hours in 1965).

Doing the dishes historically has nearly always fallen to the women of the household. But, many ladies today find that arrangement old fashioned at best. In a recent study from the University of Utah and the Council of Contemporary Families, the washing up was found to have been a major stressor when it comes to relationships between men and women.

Women who were expected by their partners to always do the dishes were found to report lower levels of satisfaction in the relationship. On the other hand, women who said their partners helped or took turns doing the dishes were happier in their unions. Women who had help with the dishes reported better sex, fewer arguments, and overall happiness with their relationship. This has been found in studies of couples in other countriesas well.

Furthermore, the arguments around the dishes in modern homes have become some of the most distressing chore-related disagreements. Of all the chores, it was reported that doing the dishes was the one that women most wanted to be shared, making it a hot topic in many households.

21. Selfies

Is taking selfies narcissistic? The answer to that question is complicated.

Past research found significant — but relatively small — links between taking selfies and narcissism. Other research has found no substantial link. Still other research has shown a stronger link for men than women. This inconsistency in research results may be because not all selfies are equal. Research has shown that narcissistic individuals take more solo selfies, but fewer selfies that feature other people. And while researchers have focused a lot on how the frequency of selfie-taking relates to personality, few studies have really examined why people take selfies. New research by Erin Koterba and colleagues, recently published in the journal Media Psychology, examined these issues.

Narcissism is defined as a grandiose perception of the self with a desire to be admired and a lack of empathy for others. Personality questionnaires that measure narcissism can divide the trait into multiple components:

Leadership/Authority: Feeling that one is important and should be in charge of other people

Entitlement/Exploitativeness: Feeling that one is deserving of special privileges and being willing to take advantage of others

Grandiose exhibitionism: The desire to show off and be the center of attention

In the study, 276 college students completed a survey consisting of a questionnaire measuring narcissism. Then they estimated how many selfies they took in the past week, both alone and with other people in the photo. Respondents also answered an open-ended question in which they listed what motivates them to take selfies.

The results showed that one particular aspect of narcissism — grandiose exhibitionism — was the only personality trait linked to self-taking, and solo-selfies in particular. Exhibitionism wasn't related to taking selfies that included other people. However, even though this correlation was statistically significant, it wasn't that large. So grandiose exhibitionism is only one small factor that makes people more prone to taking solo selfies.

The researchers coded the open-ended responses about people's selfie-taking motives into different categories and calculated the percentage of respondents who listed each type of motive:

Narcissistic: For example, "I think I am attractive and I have no problem sharing that," 29.5%

Sharing and connecting: For example, "I want to share my experiences with my friends," 23.3%

Functional use: For example, "I am a sponsored fitness athlete. It's my job," 22.80%

Self-esteem boosting: For Example "So I can feel better about myself," 15.54"

Memory: For example, "Document memories," 5.7%

Conformity: For example, "It's what young people do, so it's just a trend I follow," 3.1%

As you can see from the list above, narcissistic motives were the most common. But sharing and connecting and functional use came in close second and third. So while almost a third of the respondents indicated narcissistic reasons for posting selfies, that still means 70% listed other reasons. Interestingly, these narcissistic motives were not linked to participants' level of narcissism.

So, if 30% of respondents had narcissistic motives for posting selfies, does that mean that young adults are narcissistic? Given that these motives were not associated with respondents' level of narcissism, it suggests something else might be going on. The researchers argue that concluding that this shows evidence of the narcissism of young people is premature. They point out that young adults tend to be more focused on themselves, but not necessarily more narcissistic. Concerns about finding your own identity and how you present yourself to other people loom large in young adulthood.

Also, the motives classified by the researchers as narcissistic may not necessarily always indicate narcissism. The researchers had to code open-ended responses and then they interpreted them as falling into one of the six motivation categories. In fact, motives reflecting the "body positivity" movement might be interpreted as narcissistic, using these methods of coding participants‘ responses, depending on how the respondents phrased their responses. Self-esteem boosting was only listed by a small number (15%) of participants as a motive for selfie-posting, but it might be that people don't consciously list that as their main reason for taking selfies, even if esteem-boosting is their underlying motive. So they might say, I post selfies because "I'm happy with my body and I want to show it off," but it means "I've worked hard to become happy with my body, and I want others to see that and feel empowered too" or "I'm finally happy with how I look, but I still need that validation from others." In fact, some research has shown that vulnerable narcissism, a form of narcissism that is more introverted where people vacillate between pride and shame, is associated with taking selfies related to physical appearance. This suggests that selfie-taking can sometimes indicate insecurity.

This research suggests that self-centered motives for taking selfies are common, but not necessarily strongly linked to trait narcissism. And narcissism's connection to selfie-taking is a small part of a bigger picture.

22. Television shopping channels

In today's world, we are spoiled with seemingly endless numbers of online streaming services and websites where we can easily start watching whatever film or TV show that tickles our fancy. It could be Netflix, HBO Max, Disney+, Peacock, or Amazon Prime Video—one does not need to look far.

Oh, and did I mention you could also go to the cinema? (Assuming cinemas are open in your area given this pandemic.)

Americans that are 18 and older spend an average of 4 hours per day watching movies and TV. In fact, Americans are the world leaders in this hobby (according to the Nielsen Total Audience Report in August 2020).

But is kicking back after work and rewatching The Office a waste of time? Does having a marathon of all eight Harry Potter movies seem totally unproductive?

One begs to differ. There are actually some benefits to watching films and TV shows.

In 2012, researchers from the University of Lancaster found that children who watched films like Harry Potter and The Chronicles of Narnia had an increase in creativity and imagination. Children who watch TV have been found to be able to construct ideas more rapidly. They were also able to express themselves more clearly than others.

Well, no surprise there. After all, a film series like Harry Potter is full of magical wonder. They're great for kids to exercise the creative side of their brains.

It Can Help Improve Your English

Okay, I can attest to this. When I was growing up, I was a huge fan of the Lord of the Rings trilogy—the films, not the books. I would re-watch all three films at least once a week. The magic, the sense of adventure, and the great action scenes really had me glued to the screens.

But, unbeknownst to me, I was also subconsciously taking in the use of the English language from it. The English dialogue that was used was so poetic and beautifully constructed. It was a great tool to use in English essays at school for a 10-year-old boy. The key here is that people, especially young children and non-English speakers, are able to actually hear how the language is used.

Yes, reading to improve your English does help, but listening to spoken words, hearing how sentences are constructed, and knowing how certain words are actually pronounced phonetically are much better ways to improve one's English.

It Can Reduce Stress

There's nothing wrong with kicking back on a Sunday afternoon after a long week and popping on an Adam Sandler movie—or any other kind of film for that matter.

Research has shown that many films can have a positive impact on a person. When someone watches a film and gets invested in the story arc of the main characters—where a conflict is resolved, or the main protagonist triumphs over the villain, or when the school nerd gets to go to prom with the cheerleading captain—it can invoke positive emotions within the viewer, thus helping them cope with the harsh realities of life.

When a person enjoys a movie, they get a hit of dopamine, which acts as a natural opioid that is responsible for feelings of happiness and pleasure.

23. Emptying the bins

24. Paying bills

7 tips to help you pay your bills on time

Make a list of your bills and their due dates, set up auto payments when possible, and sign up for reminders. Use these and other tips to help you pay your bills on time, build a positive bill payment history and support your credit health.

From mortgages to car payments to cellphone bills, most of us probably have more monthly bills than we'd prefer.

Because many creditors share your payment information with the three major consumer credit bureaus — Equifax, Experian and TransUnion — falling behind on your bills could negatively affect your credit scores.

Making late payments could also lead to late fees and penalty (higher) APRs on credit cards. Read on for some tips that can help you make your payments on time.

1. Make a list of every bill

It's almost impossible to pay all of your bills on time if you don't know all of your obligations — so identifying all your creditors, vendors and service providers can be a good place to start.

If you have a lot of bills to pay, some can fall through the cracks. To help avoid this, check your credit reports and list every lender (leave out accounts that are paid off). Next, review recent bank and credit card statements to add any recurring obligations to your list. This could include gym memberships, cellphone bills, media subscriptions, online services (like music or other apps) and utility bills.

Your list should include the lender or service provider, the minimum monthly payment and total balance due. Once you've got your list, consider separating bills into two categories: those that can be paid automatically and those that can't.

2. Find out when your payments are due

Once you've got a list of bills to pay, find out when each bill is due and add that to your list. If your due dates are all over the place, you may want to tweak them to make tracking payments easier.

Many creditors allow you to pick or change the date you pay, so go online or call to find out.

While changes may take a few billing cycles to go into effect, having the same due date for multiple bills can simplify your life. And it can be helpful to set up your bills for right after payday if you're concerned about overspending and not having enough money left to pay them later.

3. Add your payments to a calendar

Tracking your bills' due dates through a calendar or other system can come in handy.

For example, if you use an online calendar, you can add payments there. It's usually easy to add recurring events, and your calendar app may have handy tools (like color coding), so due dates stand out from other events.

4. Decide how much you want to pay

For some of your bills, you may have to pay a set amount. Others — including credit cards — may allow you to pay as much or as little as you want after making the minimum monthly payment.

Ideally, you'd pay the full balance due on all your bills every billing cycle, even on the credit cards and other accounts that allow you to carry a monthly balance. This may not always be possible. But for accounts that allow you to carry a balance, you may decide to pay more than the minimum to help you save on interest, avoid building up unnecessary debt or potentially become debt-free faster.

If you're going to pay an amount other than the minimum or full balance, note this on your list of bills to keep track of the situation.

What are minimum monthly payments?

A minimum monthly payment is the smallest amount of money due each month to keep your credit card account in good standing. Most banks determine the minimum payment by calculating 1% of the total balance owed.

5. Set up automated payments whenever possible

Armed with your list and your calendar, it's time to set up your payment system.

One approach is to pay as many bills as possible automatically.

When you set up automated payments through creditors, you can specify whether you want them to debit the minimum due, the full balance due or another amount (if the accounts allow it).

While many lenders accept automated payments from bank accounts, you may also have another option for certain monthly obligations —

charging your regular bills to one of your credit cards.

But it's best to use a credit card to pay your monthly bills only if you're confident you can afford to pay the card on time and in full. Otherwise you may build up a balance that will charge you interest — and that could undermine your efforts to stay on top of your bills.

6. Devise a system for manual payments

While it can be a good idea to autopay as much as you can, you may not be able to pay everything automatically — or you may not want to. So for those bills you pay manually, you can set up a separate system.

Pay your bills immediately. If you take this approach, the goal is to pay the bill right away. You can go online and make a payment as soon as your statement posts or bill arrives — or you can sit down and write the check, put it in an envelope and drop it in the mail the next time you go out.

Pay your bills on a certain day each month. If you don't want to jump online every time you get a bill or stop what you're doing to write a check, you can set aside a regular, recurring time to pay your bills. It may help to schedule a block of time on your calendar. But even if you take a less formal approach, try to make it part of your routine.

7. Sign up for reminders

Whether you autopay or handle bills manually, it's helpful to be reminded when bills come due.

You can remind yourself to make a payment or to check if an automatic payment cleared.

Your own calendar reminders may be enough. Another approach is to use a specialized app for organizing your money and reminding you about bills. You may also be able to sign up for alerts directly with creditors and vendors.

25. Delayed trains

There are plenty of things one can do in order to enjoy long train trips such as listen to music, read a book, or take some time to get inner peace. Check out our 7 great ideas for things to do on the train.

1. Socialize

A great time to meet new friends and interesting people is when traveling with FlixTrain. Combine two great things at the same time: traveling and making friends. Friendships usually result from common interests and similarities in personality and a train ride with FlixTrain actually demonstrates this: You are going to the same destination, you have the same approach to life, and you enjoy traveling by train. Even if your seat neighbor is not the same age as you, chances are you have a lot in common. Start a conversation and you might plant the seed for a long-lasting friendship.

Eating has always been a natural way of bringing people together so why not check out our restaurant cart. We serve refreshments such as snacks, sandwiches, coffee and soft drinks which are best enjoyed in the company of others.

2. Play games with friends

Your train trip is the perfect time to play some games with your friends. Be it traditional card games such as Go Fish, Rummy, or Crazy Eights, playing cards is something for all ages and never gets boring. For the ones with a bit darker humor and wants to share some laughs with your friends you might want to try something more modern and edgier such the famous card game Cards Against Humanity.

If you by chance are traveling alone, why not exercise your brain by doing crosswords or Sudoku? By doing crosswords you flex a very specific part of the brain that oversees your vocabulary, so doing crosswords actively help you learn new words. Wouldn't it be fun to learn some sophisticated words on the train and sound super smart when you meet your friends at your destination?

Another great idea to escape time and space is to read a good book. Bring a book on your train ride and emerge yourself into the fictional world and before you know it, you're arriving at your destination.

3. Pop in your headphones

Listen to music

Bring music with you on our train and enjoy the scenery passing by. Not only is music great for relaxation and reducing stress, it has also been found that it can make you happier, healthier and more productive. By listening to music of your own choice it can spur creativity and help completing tasks faster than if not listening to music. So, if you just want to relax or get things done on the train, music is a great tool. Check out our suggestion of great music to listen to while on the train.

Listen to podcasts

Podcasts are a great way of making time fly and there are podcasts for everything! Want to know the latest gossip in Hollywood? Are you interested in hearing experts evaluating the latest football games? Or maybe you are curious how we can be less rude to bees? Podcasts are a great way of learning about all of this. Have a look at our suggestions of the best podcasts available. Put on your headphones and enjoy the ride!

4. Watch a movie or series

Maybe the best way of making time go faster is watching a good movie or series so make sure to prepare your device for your trip. Did you know that during the time it takes between Hamburg and Cologne, you can watch the first, second and the third Harry Potter movies? And between Berlin and Stuttgart you'll generally be able to binge watch 4.5 episodes of the first season of Game of Thrones. If you don't know what to watch, here are IMDB's top 100 movies of all time. You don't have to be afraid of running out of battery on your device, there are power sockets conveniently placed next to your seat. Keep up to date with the latest movies and series on FlixTrain so you don't miss out on the hype.

5. Plan your trip

A great thing to do on the train is to plan your upcoming trip. For example, what can I do in the city? What are things I shouldn't miss? Here are some inspiring examples of what to look for in different cities.

Cologne: One thing you should definitely check out in Cologne is the Cologne Catherdral, now a UNESCO site. This massive building makes for great photos and to soak up some of the German history. Another thing the city is famous for is its beer, the Kölsch, a must try!

Stuttgart: If you're a car lover you have come to the right place! Two things you really don't want to miss are the Mercedes-Benz museum and the Porsche museum. Go and check out all the cool cars!

Berlin: Where to begin... This city has so much to offer and so many things you cannot miss. Some of the classical examples are The Berlin Wall, Brandenburger Tor, and Checkpoint Charlie. Not feeling like doing the classical tourist stuff? Then explore the vibrating nightlife and grab a falafel!

6. Meditate

While riding the train it is a great time to disconnect from the everyday life and get some peace and spend some time for yourself. Meditating has become a very popular activity in order to reduce stress, enhance self-awareness, increase focus or simply to just become more present. And the great thing is that you can practice meditation anywhere, so why not take a couple of minutes for yourself on the train? If you are meditating for the first time it may not be very easy knowing what to do, so here are some tips:

Sit or lie comfortably

Take a couple of deep breaths and close your eyes

Focus your attention on your breath and how the body moves with each inhalation and exhalation

Notice how your chest, stomach and shoulders move

If your mind wanders simply return to focusing on your natural breath

At first you can do this practice for a couple of minutes and increase the amount of time as you practice more.

7. Still got some time left?

If you, despite the above-mentioned suggestion, still got time left, consider this: Recent research suggest boredom can be something positive. Being bored is basically a result of a lack of external stimulation, there is nothing exciting or interesting happening around you. We've all been stuck in traffic at some point and gotten extremely frustrated and bored because nothing is happening. But here's the good part, when we are bored, we start thinking about things, we let our imagination wander to places it normally doesn't go. When we start thinking about things in new ways, that's when great ideas can be discovered. So, if you ever feel bored on the FlixTrain, relax, you might be minutes away from a million-dollar idea!

26. The daily commute

Nowadays, employees travel longer and longer to get to their workplace and they have to cover long distances. The daily commute is said to have an impact on our health. According to researchers, the proportion of commuters with short distances of up to five kilometres has decreased. More and more employees are covering distances of up to 50 kilometres. However, expensive rents are to blame for the fact that people have to commute every single day.

The average Londoner spends almost 50 minutes on the train, bus or other means of transport while getting to work in the morning. A study from Transport Statistics in Great Britain shows that people working in London have the longest average commute. Apparently, the level of education also determines the commuting distance. Employees with a university degree are said to commute the furthest at an average of 9 miles. It is shocking how much time we actually spend commuting.

Upsides of Commuting

We spend a lot of time commuting – almost as much time as we spend on socialising or practicing our hobbies. Who wouldn't rather spend the time on anything else than sitting on the train for hours each day? The daily commute is also said to have an impact on our physical health. However, studies over the last couple of years show that commuting can have upsides too. Especially when you have to take the public transport to get to your workplace you might be happy to find out about the upsides of commuting which will make your daily journey a little bit better.

During the last years, studies showed that people commuting on a daily basis end up being more productive at work even though people at first tend to be stressed in a crowded bus or any other public transport. While we are on our way to work in the morning, we tend to think ahead and plan our day at work. People who set their goals for the day also seem to be less stressed by travelling to work than those who travel aimlessly. This also leads to greater job satisfaction throughout the day.

The evening commute, however, can be used best to reflect on everything you achieved at work on that day. A study showed that people who reflected on their work on a daily basis usually performed 20 percent better than people who didn't. Devoting a little time to reflect on your day can help you improve your sense of achievement as well as your productivity.

For some, commuting is a good opportunity to increase their own productivity and to work through their first tasks before they arrive at work. For others, commuting is associated with stress and a reduction in well-being.

When commuting becomes working time

The boundaries between work and leisure are blurring – due to digitalisation and technology. This can have an impact on our health. More and more people are dissatisfied with their long commuting times and work-life balance. This raises the question as to whether commuting should not be counted as working time and therefore rewarded.

Up to now, commuting is not considered as working time. Thus the employer does not have to pay for these hours either as it is up to the employees how they get to their workplace.

If commuting was counted as working time, it would also have social and economic consequences. Transport would as well be affected. This could reduce traffic jams during rush hour and also give employees more comfort and flexibility with their working hours. However, it would also mean that employers would monitor their work more closely on the way to the office in order to see how commuters actually use their time on public transport.

27. Formula 1

Formula" One and the baby formulas that came later

The reason why the sport is called "Formula" One is rooted in history. Pioneer motor racing placed no limitations on the size or power of the competing cars. With technological advances, this free-for-all quickly made for ludicrously dangerous conditions — especially as the early races were fought out on public roads. As a result, the governing body of the sport at the time began imposing key limitations on the format of the cars in terms of power, weight, and size. Only cars complying with this "formula" of rules could compete. The rules of Grand Prix racing have adapted to the technology and needs of the times. The rules formulated for racing immediately after World War II were given the tag of "Formula One", a name that has stuck ever since. Formula Two was invented shortly afterwards as a junior category, with a smaller engine capacity. Not long after that, Formula Three came into being for even smaller single-seaters. The Formula Two name was dropped in the mid-1980s and replaced by Formula 3000, denoting the cubic centimeter capacity of the engines. Formula Three remains. If illogical and inconsistent labelling bugs you, motor racing is not for you.

The premiere racing sport in the world

Formula One stands at the technological pinnacle of all motorsport. It's also the richest, most intense, most difficult, most political, and most international racing championship in the world. Most of the world's best drivers are either there or aspire to be there, and the same goes for the best designers, engineers, engine builders, and so on. It's a sport that takes no prisoners: Under-achievers are spat out with ruthless lack of ceremony. Formula One takes its position at the top of the motorsport tree very seriously.

Formula One traces its lineage directly back to the very beginnings of motor racing itself, at the end of the nineteenth century, when public roads were the venues. All other racing series have sprung up in its wake.

Comparing Formula One and other types of racing

Racing in America for a time overlapped in its development with European racing; then it veered off in the direction of oval track racing.

CART and IRL racing in America

Formula racing in America became Indy Car racing, spawning the CART and IRL series of today. These cars look like Formula One cars to a casual onlooker, but a Formula One car is lighter, more agile, and more powerful. Another difference is that Formula One cars never race on ovals; instead they race on purpose-built road racing tracks or street circuits. Furthermore, each Formula One team designs and builds its own cars rather than buy them off the shelf from a specialist producer.

NASCAR and Touring Car racing

Non-formula, road car-based racing spawned NASCAR in America and Touring Car racing in the rest of the world. Both are for cars that from the outside look like showroom road-going models but which underneath the skin are very different. NASCAR tailors to American production models and races mainly — though not exclusively — on ovals. Touring cars are based on European or Australian road cars and, like F1 cars, race on road racing or street tracks.

The feeder formulas

In Europe, feeder formulas to Formula One — where drivers, team owners, designers, and engineers can all hone their craft on the way to Formula One — developed. Today these are classed as Formula 3000 and Formula 3. The names and numbers have changed over the years, but Formula One remains what it has always been — the pinnacle. F3 is currently for single-seater cars with engines based on road-going production cars not exceeding 2-liter capacity. F3000 is for single seaters powered by a specific 3-liter racing engine defined by the governing body.

28. New mums on Facebook who constantly upload pictures of their baby

You haven't showered in a few days, and you haven't brushed your teeth yet this morning.

But, your baby is one month old today! You picked out the perfect outfit and made sure the lighting was just right for the perfect photo. You posted the best one on Facebook this morning, and you keep checking to see if anyone has "liked" the picture.

But, after scrolling through the "likes" and comments, you notice that your mother-in-law, who is always online, hasn't responded to the picture of her darling grandbaby yet.

Why not? What gives? Perhaps she didn't see it yet...or maybe she doesn't like the baby's outfit. Maybe she thinks you're not a good mother.

And what about that friend of yours from high school? You always "like" and comment on the photos of her kids...why hasn't she acknowledged your baby's photo? Perhaps you aren't such a good mother after all.

To some, this scenario might sound ridiculous, but it is a real and frequent consequence of being a new mother and sharing on Facebook.

So, when one of my graduate students approached me about creating and including a survey about new parents' social networking in my latest parenting study, the New Parents Project, I jumped at the chance. I was interested in how often new parents used social networking sites, why some used them more than others, and what the impact might be on new parents' mental health. Here are some things we found.

Why would a busy and exhausted new mother use valuable time to craft the perfect baby photo for Facebook? Moreover, why should she care so much about how these "friends"—some of whom are family and close friends, but many of whom are mere acquaintances —respond to photos of her baby?

To connect. Being a new mother can be lonely and overwhelming.

When I joined Facebook in 2008, my daughter was past the baby stage, but I noticed immediately that Facebook was littered with photos and posts about babies and young children.

I was by no means the first or the only person to recognize this phenomenon. Parent "overshare" on Facebook prompted the launch of the "STFU, parents" humor site in 2009.

I also joined right in. I found myself increasingly focused on capturing the perfect images of my daughter's accomplishments and adventures and anxiously awaiting the stream of likes and comments that would give me the boost I needed as I struggled to manage parenting a toddler while working full-time.

I didn't always feel boosted.

When pride becomes a downer

Our study looked at new parents' use of Facebook. It followed 182 dual-earner couples who were expecting their first child across the year surrounding their transition to parenthood.

When their babies were nine months old, we surveyed these mothers and fathers about their use of Facebook and other social networking sites in the early months of parenthood.

We asked our questions of fathers as well as of mothers, but we quickly discovered that mothers were the ones spending more time on social networking sites and taking primary responsibility for posting baby photos. Thus, we focused our research on new mothers.

One of the first things we discovered was that certain mothers—specifically, those who were more concerned with others validating their identities as mothers and those who believed that others expect them to be perfect parents—were more active on Facebook. They reported stronger emotional reactions when posted photos of their child received more or fewer likes and comments than anticipated.

We then tested whether Facebook use was associated with elevated depressive symptoms in the first months of parenthood. Indeed, we found that mothers who were more prone to seek external validation for their mothering identity and were perfectionistic about parenting experienced increases in depressive symptoms indirectly through higher levels of Facebook activity. Moreover, greater Facebook activity was also linked to elevated parenting stress for new mothers.

Inevitable comparisons bring stress

How might greater Facebook use lead new mothers to feel stressed and blue?

A related study may provide an answer. Based on survey data from 721 mothers, Sarah Coyne from Brigham Young University and her colleagues reported that mothers who more frequently compared themselves to others on social networking sites felt more depressed, more overloaded in the parental role, and less competent as parents.

The authors noted that people tend to portray themselves in a highly positive manner on social networking sites. This may be particularly true for mothers, who can feel pressured to be perfect parents.

If you are comparing yourself to others' seemingly perfect images of parenting and family life, you may inevitably come up short. This may be especially true for new mothers whose experiences have gone differently than expected. Think about the new mother who was determined to have a natural birth but ended up having a cesarean section, or the new mother whose child was born premature or with a developmental disability.

Thus, it may not merely be time spent on social networking sites, but rather how mothers spend their time on these sites and whether mothers compare themselves to others that may ultimately affect mothers' adjustment to parenthood and well-being.

Even though my research and that of others has highlighted the perils of social networking sites, other studies have shown that social networking can benefit mothers through maintaining and strengthening relationships with family and friends. And, my own work found that mothers for whom a greater proportion of Facebook "friends" are family members or relatives experience greater parenting satisfaction.

However, I think mothers should carefully consider their motivations for using Facebook and their reactions to Facebook activity. If you find you are obsessing over "likes" on your photos, consider turning off notifications on Facebook and logging on only at certain times of the day.

Or, if time spent on Facebook leaves you feeling blue, you may benefit from taking a "break" from Facebook for weeks or months and instead focus on making phone calls to long-distance friends and meeting local ones face-to-face for coffee.

All parents who use Facebook and other social networking sites can help too by working harder to share the struggles as well as the triumphs of parenting. They can also support instead of criticize mothers who portray themselves in a less-than-perfect—but more authentic—light.

29. Social media challenges

15 Most Dangerous Social Media Challenges to Avoid

Humans are social animals with an innate desire for attention. Social media capitalizes on this need, which is why people love joining viral "challenges."

Some of these challenges — like the mannequin challenge and the trashtag challenge — are admittedly awesome. Others are just plain silly. Worse, many social media trends have proven to be dangerous and even deadly.

These are the most dangerous social media challenges.

Back in March 2020, there were still many people who did not take coronavirus seriously. Springbreakers rushed to Florida taking advantage of cheap tickets, not long before realizing the global pandemic would be much more serious than they thought.

Another person who thought it was a joke was Ava Louise, an influencer highly lacking in common sense as well as basic personal hygiene. As a desperate ploy to get followers, she filmed herself licking an airplane toilet seat in what she called the "coronavirus challenge."

Marketing on social media has changed from a nice-to-have to a must-have for modern brands. The power of social can be gauged from these facts:

Daily, 45% of the world devotes 2 hours 24 minutes to social media.

73% of marketers consider social media marketing effective.

Social media ads are driving purchase decisions for almost 80% of people.

Whether you're an expert or a rookie at social media marketing, you will agree with us that it isn't easy. Changing technological and social trends make it very challenging. Additionally, there are difficulties in strategy formulation, ROI measurement, and allocation of time and budget.

In this post, we cover five of the most common social media marketing challenges that marketers face and actionable solutions to overcome them.

Top 5 Social Media Marketing Challenges (and Their Solutions)

Social media marketing can be a mystery if you are unfamiliar with the way it works. By understanding its challenges, you can cope with them better. You can draft your strategy, use the right tools, and tweak your approach accordingly.

Challenge #1: Defining Marketing Goals

It's surprising how many marketers struggle with goal setting for their marketing campaigns. Marketers face difficulties in creating social marketing strategies that align with the goals of their business. 47% of them cite this as their biggest challenge.

While increased brand awareness remains a top goal for 70% of marketers, many are still unclear about which KPIs matter.

If your goals are not well-defined, you will find it hard to measure your marketing performance and demonstrate its value to your stakeholders. This can adversely affect the budget for your future campaigns.

Solution

Start with big-picture goals. Ask yourself, why your business is on social media. This exercise will help you identify the business objectives you hope to meet through social media marketing. Then, you can go about planning your social media marketing goals.

Next, set SMART goals for each campaign. SMART stands for specific, measurable, attainable, realistic, and time-bound. SMART goals keep your campaigns on-track and prevent you from deviating from the set budget.

Specific: The kind of engagement, platform, and target area should be well defined.

Measurable: You can use the analytics of each social media platform to measure your reach and engagement.

Attainable: Ensure that the goal can be met by organic and paid campaigns.

Realistic: Set a goal that you can actually achieve in a specific time frame. Use your past performance as a benchmark.

Time-bound: The time frame should be well-defined to help you compute accurate metrics.

The SMARTer your goals, the more effective your campaign. Plus, you can measure your KPIs against your goals and get buy-in from your management for your next budget.

Challenge #2: Identifying the Right Platform

The next hurdle marketers face is in the selection of which platforms to leverage. Few marketers research their target markets thoroughly enough to identify the platforms where their target audience is active.

From the chart below, there seems to be a disconnect between customers and marketers. You can see that LinkedIn is used by 38% of social media marketers whereas only 6% of consumers use the platform to follow brands. This means marketers are wasting their efforts and resources on platforms that are not bankable.

Investing in the wrong platforms can exhaust your budget, especially if you regularly use paid ads. If the decision-makers in your company are not sold on the idea of social media marketing in the first place, they might just pull the plug if you commit this misstep.

Solution

In a way, if you overcome the first challenge of goal setting, you are well on your way to overcoming this challenge too.

For example, if you want to establish a personal connection with customers, Twitter is your best bet. On the other hand, Instagram is great if you want to leverage influencers to spread brand awareness.

However, if you need information on how other marketers select platforms, you can use the chart below as a benchmark:

Take the time to get to know your audience. Which platforms are they active on? What are their main activities on social media? Dissect your audience demographics to learn about their genders, ages, and locations. Then, meet them where they are active. A lot depends on the nature of your business as well. B2C brands need to be active on visual platforms like Facebook and Instagram to grab the attention of consumers.

B2B brands can benefit from local SEO on Google My Business and Bing. They should also post regularly on LinkedIn to make useful connections with brands. You also need to keep tabs on your competitors. "Out of sight, out of mind," is very true for social media users. If you don't have a strong presence on channels that your competitors are acing, you're bound to lose a lot of conversion opportunities.

Social media listening can help you track the brand mentions of your competitors. Identify the channels where they are garnering attention. Then, plan outreach on those channels.

Challenge #3: Understanding the Target Audience

There are many brands that do superb business in-store but fail miserably on social. The difference is that in brick-and-mortar stores, customers approach brands, whereas, on social media, brands have to seek out customers. And, do some brands have no clue how to do this.

Too often, marketers create content first and figure out the target audience later. They have the misconception that great content converts, even if it is not targeted. Though great content gets engagement, it might not generate leads if it isn't tailored to your target audience's needs.

Directionless marketing relies on a spray-and-pray approach that seldom gives the desired returns. In fact, it can damage your brand's credibility. You run the risk of getting blocked or reported if you bombard people with irrelevant content.

Solution

Do you know who your ideal customer is? Have you created a precise buyer persona? Dig into your existing customer base, ad analytics, and email subscriber list. Create a fictional customer avatar from the data you collect.

Get personal with the data. How many kids does your customer have? How do they spend their weekends? What kind of music do they love? Gather as many insights as are relevant to your business.

You can use social listening tools to capture insights. You can drill down into customer conversations around your brand, product, and niche. Understand the consumer sentiment and pain points to shape your campaign goals and content.

Kraft Foods used social data when they were planning to introduce mini-burgers or sliders. Using social listening, they identified slider themes popular among different customer segments. Social research guides the brand's product strategy as well. Their super-successful Mayochup was a result of one such research.

Social listening will also help you understand the "why" behind customer actions. Why are they following a particular platform? Why did they unfollow your brand? Why is your brand mention volume low? Use the insights you gathered to establish a personal connection with customers and create more appealing content.

Challenge #4: Declining Organic Reach and Engagement Rates

Organic reach on leading social platforms is plummeting. Simultaneously, the cost of paid ads is increasing. Brands are struggling to strike a balance between goals and budget.

Take a look at this chart from Trust Insights. It analyses engagement on one million posts from 4,097 brands on Instagram.

As you can see, the number is declining significantly. The median engagement rate for unpaid branded content on Instagram stands at just 0.31% now. This means if you have a follower count of 1000, only 3.1 of them will engage with your content.

Facebook defends the trend by saying that people prefer to see content from their friends and families, and not brands. But their claim falls flat as 90% of Instagrammers follow businesses too.

Brands were just coming to terms with the bad news when Facebook and Instagram rolled out new updates to help brands monetise their content. Instagram's Checkout feature is the latest addition in this series. Though the thought is great, brands have to pay a commission to the platforms. For a small business with a few hundred followers, these updates could mean near-zero organic reach.

That's not all. Instagram's influencer industry is also waning. In 2019, Trust Insights analysed the profiles of 4,462 influencers. The reported the median engagement rate for 632,379 unpaid posts fell by 41.2% in just one year.

This means that the brands will have to rely on sponsored influencer content to make their presence felt on Instagram.

Solution:

Make your platforms work for you. Know the algorithms well. If Instagram is your main platform, leverage Instagram Stories. They have great engagement rates and allow you to tell your brand's story effectively.

Going live is another simple way to maximise your organic reach. You can use IGTV if you want to broadcast long-form stories. You can collaborate with influencers to host interviews, podcasts, and interactive Q&A sessions.

Optimise your social content for the right specs and posting times. Video marketing is big these days. Use videos to showcase your knowledge and troubleshoot customers' problems. Cross-promote all your social content to grab more eyeballs organically.

Smart marketers leverage user-generated content (UGC), which can be generated free of cost. Think of ways to get your followers to share content that you can reuse on your social media accounts.

The social proof will add to your brand's credibility.

Airbnb uses this strategy and almost-exclusively posts UGC on its Instagram page.

Hashtag contests and giveaways are guaranteed to produce a lot of UGC. If you instruct followers to tag their friends, you can earn more followers and leads.

Challenge #5: Increasing Ad Cost

Brands with deep pockets may prefer to buy engagement through paid ads on social media. But even that is becoming challenging. Ad costs are increasing and competition is stiff. It's getting harder to recover your investment and make a profit from paid ads.

One reason behind this trend is the immense popularity of paid ads, especially Facebook ads. In Q3 of 2019, there were 7 million active advertisers on Facebook. With so much ad content, marketers are finding it difficult to cut through the noise and reach their targets.

Solution:

On Facebook, you have many placement options like mobile or desktop news feed, right-panel ads, messenger ads, and Facebook's Audience Network. We suggest that you opt for mobile placement since Facebook has an extensive user base among mobile users.

If you want to know more about the different ad formats and placements, go through Facebook's quarterly earnings reports. You will get a good idea about the unique ad impressions that each format garners in a day.

Returns from paid ads are measurable. So, make sure that your advertising goals are in place before you start your ad campaign. This way, you can find out if your campaign has fulfilled its goals.

Use advanced targeting to reach prospects who aren't your followers. Using the buyer persona we mentioned before, cover as many target segments as possible with your ad. Avoid overlapping audience types that just eat up your ad budget without driving returns. Facebook's Lookalike Audiences can help you zero in on your ideal customers.

Ready to Tackle These Challenges?

All types of marketing come with their own set of challenges. Social media marketing is no exception. Now that you are familiar with these issues, you are better prepared to handle them. Use the tips and strategies mentioned in this post to risk-proof your social media marketing efforts.

30. Small talk

Why Small Talk Is a Big Deal

The ability to engage in small talk is an underrated social skill.

Do you dread trading niceties with retail clerks and assorted other strangers when you are out in public? Do you go out of your way to avoid neighbors and co-workers so that you do not have to engage in idle chitchat about the weather and other equally inoffensive topics? Does your blood run cold when you receive an invitation to a cocktail party?

If this sounds like you, then you have an aversion to small talk.

Small talk is defined by the Oxford English Dictionary as "Polite conversation about unimportant or uncontroversial matters, especially as engaged in on social occasions."

Some people hate small talk because they perceive it as a waste of time and as an impediment to a meaningful conversation; others may hate it simply because they are not good at it.

How you feel about small talk depends to some extent on where you are from. Stereotypically, Americans are more tolerant of small talk than people from other places and expect to encounter it in social situations. Scandinavians, on the other hand, are more comfortable with awkward silences than with awkward small talk, and the British TV show Very British Problems devoted an entire episode to the excruciating tactics that many Brits will resort to in an attempt to avoid small talk.

There are also consistent gender differences in how small talk plays out. While everyone likes to talk about the weather, women are also likely to compliment each other's clothing and appearance, whereas men are more likely to employ playful insults. In both cases, people are signaling a desire to establish a mutually comfortable level of involvement in the conversation.

Is There a Downside to Small Talk?

Many critiques of small talk reference a demonstration organized by Duke University Psychologist Dan Ariely as evidence that there might be some real advantages from banishing small talk from our daily lives.

Ariely arranged a dinner party for 27 guests with the following rule: No small talk allowed!

All guests were required to arrive at exactly the same time, and the hosts provided index cards with meaningful conversation starters. The guests were required to police their conversations by sounding the alarm and changing direction if they perceived that the conversation was drifting in the direction of small talk. The party turned out to be a rousing success, and those in attendance confirmed that it was one of the most interesting and stimulating social events that they had ever attended.

Small talk haters are also quick to cite a study by psychologist Mathias Mehl and his colleagues, published in Psychological Science in 2010. In Mehl's study, 79 undergraduate students wore an electronic device that recorded 30 seconds of sound every 12.5 minutes for four days. Afterward, all of the captured conversations were categorized as either small talk or as substantive, meaningful conversation. His participants completed a battery of questionnaires designed to measure happiness and well-being, and it turned out that higher levels of well-being were associated with less small talk and more substantive conversation.

One of the conclusions that many drew from these results was that engaging in small talk diminishes one's well-being.

However, Mehl repeated the study in 2018 with a much larger sample and a more sophisticated analysis of the data, and this time concluded that small talk does not undermine happiness and that it is associated with more happiness than one usually experiences when one is alone. In other words, it is better to engage in small talk than to engage in no talk at all. The results of the earlier study apparently reflected the strong positive effect that meaningful conversation has on happiness rather than any negative effects of small talk.

In recent years, small talk has been belatedly recognized as a beneficial feature of everyday life. For example, studies indicate that people are happier when they talk to others, even if it is just strangers on a subway, and even if it is just small talk.

The problem with many previous discussions of small talk was a framing of the issue as a contest between the benefits of small talk versus the benefits of deeper conversation as if people must be forced to engage in only one or the other.

The trick is to be skillful in the use of both types of talk in your social interactions. Rather than being antagonistic to each other, these different types of talk are strategies that work in tandem to create effective relationships.

Yes, of course, you are bound to be disappointed if all of your conversations are nothing more than superficial loops of chatter about things that no one really cares about; but the skilled conversationalist knows how to use small talk as a social lubricant and as a segue to deeper topics. Think of small talk as a tool that negotiates and defines a relationship. It can be a way of synchronizing the level of intimacy felt by each of the partners in the conversation and a way of signaling friendly intentions while simultaneously minimizing awkward, uncomfortable silences.

The actual topics of small talk do not matter very much; its purpose is not to convey information, but rather to serve as an opening act to warm up the audience for the meaty stuff to follow.

In short, being adept with small talk is an important component of your arsenal of social skills. Knowing when to initiate small talk and also knowing when to move on and escalate the level of discourse beyond the mundane will make you a popular conversational partner.

And always be careful not to overstep the level of intimacy inherent in a situation, especially when the small talk strays into the realm of personal topics such as health or physical appearance.

31. Changing a duvet cover

Changing a duvet cover seems simple in theory, but it can be a hassle trying to fit a puffy duvet in through small duvet cover opening. Changing a duvet cover is not unlike putting a pillowcase onto a pillow, except for the fact that a duvet doesn't have the firmness of a pillow and it tends to twist inside the cover. While changing a duvet can be a challenge, there are a couple changing methods that can ease the process, especially if you're working alone.

Lay the duvet on the bed. Lay the duvet comforter flat on the mattress so it is all spread out.[1] Be sure that the long side of the duvet is running lengthwise on the bed, and the shorter side of the duvet is running the width of the bed. Also make sure that the tag on the duvet is at the head of the bed.

Having the tag at the head of the bed will ensure that the tag ends up at the bottom of the duvet cover when you insert the duvet into the cover.

Turn the duvet cover inside out. Stand at the foot of the bed and spread the duvet cover out and on top of the duvet, with the open end of the duvet cover near you. This doesn't have to be perfectly neat, just spread out enough that you can see the different corners of the duvet cover. Reach your hands into the duvet cover through the bottom opening.[2] Reach until you can grab onto the two top corners of the cover near the head of the bed.

Grab the left corner with your left hand, and the right corner with your right hand. Pull these two inside corners toward you, out through the duvet cover opening, to turn the cover inside out.[3]

Once the duvet cover is turned inside out, once again lay it over the duvet with the opening of the cover near you.

Grab the corners of the duvet. With the duvet cover inside out, once again reach through the cover opening to grab onto the two top corners of the cover.[4] Once you have a hold on the top two corners of the duvet cover, bring your hands down near the end of the bed to grab onto the bottom two corners of the actual duvet comforter.[5]

Your hands should look like you're wearing mittens as your grab the bottom two corners of the duvet.

This would be the time that you would fasten any closures that the duvet or duvet cover has so the corners of the duvet stay in place within the cover while you use the blanket. These closures might be buttons or some sort of tying arrangement.

You may have to momentarily remove your hands from inside the duvet cover to fasten these closures. Once they are fastened, you can reinsert your hands into the cover.

Shake the duvet cover onto the duvet. Through the duvet cover's two top corners, hold tightly onto the two bottom corners of the actual duvet. Flip the duvet cover over your hands while still holding onto the duvet corners, and shake the cover on to the duvet.[6]

Be sure to hold on tight as you shake the duvet cover onto the duvet. This will help ensure that all corners of the duvet are spread out to all corners inside the duvet cover.

Powerfully shake the duvet and duvet cover as if you are trying to wave a blanket evenly onto a bed.[7]

You can also stand on the edge of the bed and hold the top two corners of the duvet and duvet cover, to evenly shake the cover over the duvet.

You may have to pull the last portion of the cover over the bottom of the duvet and tuck in the corners.Spread the duvet onto the bed. Once the duvet is completely inside the duvet cover, fasten the inside closures on the two bottom corners of the duvet and duvet cover (if your duvet and duvet cover have any). Once the inside closures are secure, you can close the duvet cover opening at the foot of the bed.[8]

Give your duvet a little shake and pull on all side to make sure the duvet is spread out evenly.

32. Waiting for a train

33. Phone calls that could be quick emails

34. Looking for a parking space

35. Company-wide emails

36. Filling tax returns

37. Horse racing

38. PowerPoint presentations

39. Places without Wi-Fi

40. Trailing around behind your partner in a clothes shop

41. Dieting

42. Waiting for your phone to recharge

43. Waiting for the oven to heat up

44. Rice cakes

45. Ed Sheeran

46. Gardener's World

47. People telling you about their dream

48. Working overtime for no extra pay

49. Replacing the toilet roll on the holder

50. Bargain Hunt

CHAPTER SIX

Why Am I So Boring?

STORYTIME: Why Am I So Boring?- How I let my fear of being boring rob me of fulfilling experiences.

For as long as I can remember, I've worried about what others thought of me and struggled with the insecurity that I was a dull, boring and uninteresting person.

I'm convinced it's one of the many reasons why I was painfully shy, especially around groups of people.

I know you're not supposed to care what other people think. But let's face it, that's easier said than done, and some of us (myself included) do care.

Sure everyone has felt shy at one point or another in their life, but I was shy and nervous to the point that It was debilitating.

These fears and insecurities weren't rational. They had power over me, made me feel inadequate and stopped me from living my life to the fullest simply because I didn't want to let the world see my boring self.

Are you an Empath?

A friend of mine recently suggested that I might be an "empath." Not the kind of person that can read minds. That's what I thought she meant at first too.

An empath, according to Dr. Judith Orloff, a pioneer in the field, is someone who absorbs the world's joys and stresses like "emotional sponges."

After doing some research, I might be an empath? It makes sense because I've always had an unusually high sensitivity to outside stimuli, big personalities, and hectic environments. I tend to feel things very deeply, while others around me could care less. These feelings control how I behaved around others, control my emotions and stress me out.

For example:

I tried to make myself invisible, withdrew from activities and felt anxious in most social settings.

I had an irrational fear of being observed and evaluated by others.

I used to lunch, in school and later when I began working, with co-workers.

It became normal for me to shrink into the background.

I agonized over what to say in conversations and ended up saying nothing.

I felt awkward in social settings.

I was envious of other people, with their fascinating personalities, laughing and having fun, while all I could feel was anxiety and fear.

These childhood struggles and worries left their mark on my life and scarred part of my soul, but they also helped shape who I am today.

I highly recommend the book" 'The empaths survival guide: life strategies for sensitive people.

I changed the narrative by identifying and facing my fears.

It wasn't until I was a teenager and moved to Montreal to live with my aunt to attend Highschool that I made the conscious effort to tackle these worries and insecurities.

I was in a new city, a new school, a new setting, and I didn't know anyone except my aunt, uncle and cousins. A situation that was scary in and of itself but at the same time, I saw it as an opportunity to reinvent myself.

I didn't have a psychologist or self-help books, so I did the only thing I could.

I adopted a "fake it till you make it attitude."

It's like that famous quote, "do one thing every day that scares you."

My life started to change after that, and some of my fondest memories were during this period when I learned to feel better in my own skin. That's when I first realized and acknowledged that my irrational fears of being boring were controlling my life.

I still feel those fears; it never goes away; however, I've learned to manage them.

My friends today are surprised that I feel shy and secure inside.

I'm a grown woman now, married with three children.

People who know me have a hard time believing I was ever a shy or insecure person who worried if other people thought I was boring.

I owe it all to one simple thing:

By facing my fears and insecurities, I was facing my bully, acknowledging its presence but not letting it have power over me. I had to do a lot of things outside of my comfort zone. By doing so, I built courage and achieved personal growth.

Conquering my fears gave me the courage to suck the marrow out of life. Without these experiences, I might not have moved to France, Eloped to Scotland, or moved to Japan when I was 18 years old and lived there for 3.5 years.

I'm still not the life of the party, but that's ok.

I would love to tell you that I completely overcame my insecurities, but the truth is, I still feel remnants of those old childhoods and young adult pangs of shyness. The fear that other people will think I'm a boring person sometimes creeps back into my head, even to this day.

The difference is it's not debilitating anymore, and I don't let those fears stop me from experiencing my life or compromise my life goals.

10 Signs You're A Boring Person And How To Be Less Boring!

Enough about me. I won't bore you with any more personal details; no pun intended.

The first step in overcoming some of your fears about being a boring person is recognizing that these are irrational fears. You're not a boring person!

Here are the top 10 things that I feared the most and how I conquered these fears.

1-You Talk Non-Stop About Things That Only Interest You.

I'm not a natural-born chatterbox, and I don't have the gift of the gab, but I noticed that some of the people I admired most talked a lot, so I tried it—bad Idea.

I ended up droning on and on, talking only for the sake of talking. It was both exhausting and unnatural. I probably bored the other person to death because nothing screams BORING more than being on the receiving end of a one-sided conversation, listening to someone talk non-stop about a subject you couldn't care less about.

Sign: if you notice you're doing all the talking and the other person has gone quiet, it might be a sign the other person is not interested or engaged.

Solution: It's still a work in progress, but I've since learned there's an art to having a mutually beneficial and interesting conversation. Try engaging with the person you're talking to by asking them questions. Listen to them and genuinely be interested in what they have to say. Read books about being a magnificent storyteller.

Your ability to have interesting and meaningful conversations will not only help develop your people skills; it will improve your life.

2- You're A Total Downer

If you've ever watched Saturday Night Live, you probably know the character "Debbie downer."

"Debbie downer" was a killjoy, dampening the mood in social settings by excessively sharing unsolicited sad and depressing remarks in every situation.

We've all been there, and that's ok, but it gets problematic if you're a chronic downer. I'm not talking about people that suffer from depression, although it can feel that way sometimes.

I never considered myself a downer until I met someone who was and saw a little of myself in this other person. It was painful to listen to this person's negative self-talk, and I didn't always know how to respond because I was dealing with my own struggles.

I wasn't a downer about life, but I often made overly self-deprecating remarks about my flaws in social situations, which I disguised as humour.

"Don't look at my face; I look like a blowfish."

I think making someone laugh was a self-defence mechanism to admit to a flaw and make light of it through laughter before someone else could notice or say something.

Sign: You always see the negative or have a "glass half full" attitude. You may not even see yourself as a downer, but call yourself a realist.

Examples of depressing conversation killers

"Oh, you earned your bachelor's degree? I wish I finished my degree; I can't get a job."

"I'm taking my driver's test next week. I know I won't pass the test."

"You bought a new house? Oh my, real estate is such a bad investment."

"Jack and Jill just got married. I give it 2 years before they get a divorce."

Solution: Sometimes, life can get you down, but when life gives you lemons, make lemonade.

Make a conscious effort to see the silver lining in every situation, whether it's a lesson to be learned or something that could positively impact the future.

3- You're Really Uptight And Painfully Serious

Fun people like to laugh, tell jokes and let loose once in a while, the total opposite of an uptight person.

After my children were born, I started to become this rigid person who could never relax.

All I could see were problems everywhere, and it consumed me and oozed into other parts of my life. It made me a not-so-fun person to be around.

Sign: An uptight person is RIGID, controlling and worried about PROTOCOL. They look around, and all they see are problems and trouble instead of relaxing and having fun.

Solution: Resist your urge to be overbearing and controlling, or judgy. Pick and choose your battle and let loose once in a while. Laugh at yourself once in a while. You'll know you're having fun when you laugh and don't care who sees.

4-Your A Chronic Complainer

Complaining about everything is a little bit like being uptight. No one wants to be around someone who complains about everything.

I've been on both the giving and receiving end.

When I was on the receiving end, I realized that it's hard to remain upbeat, motivated and positive amid a constant stream of complaints. All I wanted to do was get the hell out of there. There's no joy in being around someone like this because you feel like you have to walk on eggshells around them.

Solution: Chronic complainers feel as if the world has given them the short end of the straw. They're just responding" appropriately" to the world and aggravating circumstances.

If someone tells you that you complain and criticize too much, you may disagree with that person. Many chronic complainers don't see themselves as negative, even though this is how everyone else perceives them.

Listen, take a step back and examine your motives for complaining. There is usually another underlying reason or desire underneath all the criticizing and complaining. As you notice what you're feeling, take action and do something about it.

She's so ugly": Is it validation you need?

You never spend any time with me! Is it a shared connection or more shared time that you're seeking with that other person?

"Stop walking on the grass; you're crushing it": Do you feel the need to control or feel like things are out of your control?

"Our manager is terrible at ...": Are you too afraid to directly deal with a problem about an ongoing issue, so you feel the need to vent?

5-You Rarely Try New Things or Travel To New Places

Fun people tend to get out there in life and do things.

Without life experiences, what do we talk about?

By putting yourself out there, you have the added benefit of having more experiences outside of work, which means you might have more to talk about.

"Life without adventure would be deadly dull."

Sir Robert Baden-Powell, founder and first Chief Scout of the worldwide Boy Scout

Sign: Not everyone has the time, money or inclination to get out there and suck the marrow out of life.

When my boys were young, money was tight, and I barely had enough time to do the bare essentials; work, take care of my children, cook and clean. When I did have the time, I didn't have the money and couldn't afford to pay for a sitter. To say that it was hard for me to get out there, try new things and have a life is an understatement.

Looking back, I should have tried harder or made more time to do things outside of my routine. I always had an excuse.

Solution: Make time, even if only once in a blue moon, to do something out of the ordinary — anything, big or small.

Tackle something on your bucket list (even if it's as small as reading a book)

Go to the museum or a local art gallery.

Check out a new ethnic restaurant.

Go to the gym, start knitting, teach yourself to code.

Travel to new places.

6- You Never Ever Smile

People used to constantly ask me, "Is everything ok, Annie? You look upset or angry!"

I had this permanent furrowed look on my face as if I was concentrating on solving some impossible problem. In reality, it was probably my anxiety showing through, and then it just became my face in its natural state. I had to work really hard on my facial expressions.

Sign: I picture scowling faces and furrowed eyebrows when I think of a dull and grumpy person. Which one are you? All Smiles or all frowny?

Solution: When I think about fun or happy people in my life, I picture them smiling, laughing and just being jovial. The simple act of smiling can not only lift the spirits of another person but also your own. Smiling is also contagious. The next time you make eye contact with someone, smile at them and see what happens. I once had someone stop to "thank me" for smiling at them. Try it; it works.

7- You're Super Predictable and Never Spontaneous

I love seeing life through my children's eyes because, like most kids, they are naturally curious and seek out new experiences.

It's also fun to be around adults with these qualities.

Sign: Here are some examples of some ways you can be predictable.

Everything you do has to be planned to the "T." (I'm a big planner, but I have a spontaneous side now too)

You always take the practical, safe route in life. (The key is balance. Take risks, wear a sexy dress, go to a rave, try something outside your comfort zone)

You say NO more than you say YES.

Solution: If you're stuck in a rut or dissatisfied with certain aspects of your life, try being more spontaneous. Mix things up a bit. Sometimes, I force myself to get out and do something new, even when I don't feel like it. I'm always glad I did in the end. There's something satisfying about getting out there and trying new things, even If they're outside your comfort zone.

Start right now. Go and find something new to do and say "YES" more often to new opportunities. Stop planning everything. It's hard, I know.

8- You Work All The Time

I'm all for working hard, but if that's all you do, your family and friends might disown you.

Sign: When you make work your life's purpose, you're almost guaranteed to become a boring person. I used to be so hung up on climbing the corporate ladder. It consumed me and my life. Who wants to hang out with someone who enjoys working more than they like laughing and having fun. I still work hard, but now I try to play just as hard.

Solution: Spend more time outside of work. I'm not talking about vegging out in front of the T.V. like some tired, overworked couch potato. I'm talking about living your life to the fullest and doing all those things you've always wanted to do but haven't. Don't let work define who you are. Unless, of course, you're lucky enough to have a job that is also your passion. I imagine artists and athletes might be in this category.

9-You have No Hobbies Or Passions

I love drawing in photoshop and illustrator, yoga, learning the Ukelele, crafts and DIY. I look forward to these things, which I think make me more interesting to others, especially those that share my interests. It gives us common things to talk about and bond over.

Sign: You don't go out much. You have no drive to do anything beyond working, eating and sleeping.

Solution: Get a hobby, get out there and meet other people who enjoy that same hobby.

When you're passionate about a subject, sport, hobby or pastime, it becomes part of who you are. It can give you purpose and make you feel more fulfilled. Certain hobbies also benefit from putting you in contact with other people who share the same passion as you- sailing, golfing, knitting club, mine-craft group, cooking and even board games.

10-You're A loner or boring Hermit

There's a certain stigma to being a loner.

Even so, I've always preferred solitude over social situations; it's what feels comfortable.

I'm pretty comfortable with being a loner up to a certain point, mainly because spending time in my own company has helped me understand many things about myself.

Unfortunately, the long-lasting psychological effects of living like a loner are feeling lonely or isolated at times. There's a reason why solitary confinement in prisons is a punishment. We are social beings.

In 2015, researchers from Brigham Young University looked at multiple studies on loneliness and isolation involving several hundred thousand people. They found that social isolation resulted in a 50 percent increase in premature death and increased stress and cortisol levels.

Health reasons aside, I found that when I feel lonely and isolated, it affects my mood and personality in social settings.

I never know what to talk about. I feel awkward and out of practice in social situations, which only adds to my anxiety that I'm boring the other person.

Sign:

Being a loner is not bad; however, being a loner may not be by choice if it causes you to feel lonely and isolated.

Ask yourself this:

a) Are you a loner by choice? Someone who happily prefers the comfort of their own company over social interactions?

b) Or are you a forced loner: Someone who identifies as a loner but feels isolated and lonely?

Solution:

If you're a happy loner who never feels lonely or isolated, and it never affects your mood in social situations, good for you.

If you're a loner who feels lonely and isolated: The solution for me, at least, is not so much forcing myself to get out into more social situations; it's choosing the right activities and people that motivate me to do it.

More often than not, when I force myself to get out and socialize, I always feel glad after the fact. I don't necessarily like every social situation, but throughout the years, I've found that there are certain social situations that I would do again, while others give me anxiety. But even those situations that give me anxiety become less stressful with more practice.

I still consider myself a loner and prefer the company of myself and my family, but I've struck a balance by choosing which social interactions bring me the most joy. I've found that I have more confidence and more to talk about when I don't feel lonely and depressed.

In people who are prone to boredom, this state can negatively affect their mental health. So, what happens in the brain when we get bored, and how can this help us find ways of dealing with boredom? A new study investigates.

Share on Pinterest

What happens in the brains of people who are prone to boredom? New research finds out.

On average, adults in the United States experience 131 days of boredom per year — at least that is what a recent commercial survey suggests.

What matters, though, is not just how much time a person spends feeling bored, but also how they react to the state of boredom.

Traditionally, boredom gets a bad rap because many people believe that the state of boredom equates with a lack of productivity or focus on a given task.

However, some research has indicated that it is good to be bored because this state helps boost creativity.

One way or the other, boredom is something we all have experienced repeatedly throughout our lives, and according to some research, it seems that animals might share this experienceTrusted Source with us, too.

"Everybody experiences boredom," says Sammy Perone, who is an assistant professor at Washington State University in Pullman. However, he adds, "some people experience it a lot, which is unhealthy."

For this reason, Perone and colleagues from Washington State University decided to conduct a study focusing on what boredom looks like in the brain.

The study findings — which now appear in the journal PsychophysiologyTrusted Source — might help them identify the best ways of coping with boredom so that this state does not end up affecting mental health.

At the end of the day, "we wanted to look at how to deal with [boredom] effectively," Perone explains.

The study premises

To begin with, the research team believed there was a "hardwiring" difference in the brains of people who react negatively to boredom vs. those individuals who experience no ill effects when they are bored.

However, initial tests — using electroencephalogram (EEG) caps to measure participants' brain activity — proved them wrong.

"Previously, we thought people who react more negatively to boredom would have specific brain waves prior to being bored. But in our baseline tests, we couldn't differentiate the brain waves. It was only when they were in a state of boredom that the difference surfaced," Perone explains.

So, if there was no difference in terms of brain hardwiring, then what could explain why boredom affected some people more adversely than others? The researchers decided that the most likely explanation was individual response: some people simply reacted poorly to being bored, which could affect their well-being.

Previous research, the investigators report in their study paper, has actually suggested that individuals who are often bored are also more prone to poor mental health, and particularly to conditions such as anxiety and depression.

"People who report high levels of boredom propensity have an avoidant disposition. For example, these individuals are more likely to experience depression and anxiety," the researchers write.

Based on these premises, the researchers argue that it is possible to find ways of coping with states of boredom so that they become less likely to affect mental health. But what might these strategies be? Before they could find out, Perone and team had to solve another mystery, namely what boredom looks like in the brain.

Brain activity in those prone to boredom

For their study, the researchers recruited 54 young adult participants. The researchers asked the volunteers to fill in a survey asking questions about boredom patterns and how they reacted to feeling bored.

Then, after a baseline EEG test measuring normal brain activity, the researchers assigned the participants a tedious task: they had to turn eight virtual pegs on a screen as the computer highlighted them. This activity lasted approximately 10 minutes, during which time the researchers used EEG caps to measure participants' brain activity as they carried out the boring task.

"I've never done [this activity], it's really tedious," Perone admits. "But in researching previous experiments, this was rated as the most boring task tested. That's what we needed," he explains.

In assessing the brain wave "maps" obtained via the EEGs, the researchers looked specifically at activity levels in the right frontal and left frontal areas of the brain.

That was because these two regions become active for different reasons. The left frontal part, the researchers explain, becomes more active when an individual is looking for stimulation or distraction from a situation by thinking about something different.

Conversely, the right frontal part of the brain becomes more active when an individual experiences negative emotions or states of anxiety.

The researchers found that participants who had reported being more prone to boredom on a daily basis displayed more activity in the right frontal brain area during the repetitive task, as they became increasingly bored.

"We found that the people who are good at coping with boredom in everyday life, based on the surveys, shifted more toward the left. Those that don't cope as well in everyday life shifted more right."

Sammy Perone

'Reacting more proactively to boredom'

The team's next step is to identify clear strategies that will allow people to cope better with states of boredom. Clues have already emerged after asking participants in the current study how they dealt with the boring activity.

"We had one person in the experiment who reported mentally rehearsing Christmas songs for an upcoming concert. They did the peg turning exercise to the beat of the music in their head," says Perone.

"Doing things that keep you engaged rather than focusing on how bored you are is really helpful," he notes.

In other words, proactive thinking could be a good way of coping with boredom. The trick, however, is getting individuals to learn how to do more of this, and succumb to boredom less.

"The results of this paper show that reacting more positively to boredom is possible. Now we want to find out the best tools we can give people to cope positively with being bored," explains Perone.

"So," in future studies, he adds, "we'll still do the peg activity, but we'll give [participants] something to think about while they're doing it."

"It's really important to have a connection between the lab and the real world. If we can help people cope with boredom better, that can have a real, positive mental health impact," the researcher contends.

CHAPTER SEVEN

How to Avoid Being a Boring Person

Have you ever been called a boring person? Or have you come across someone who is highly dis-interesting? If the answer is yes, then you must suggest them to read this post.

Speaking the truth, nobody likes a boring person. If you don't pique someone's curiosity or brightens someone's day, you probably are nobody. But that doesn't mean your life has ended and you can't do anything to change it.

In this post, you will learn the top interesting ways using which you can quit being a bore and create a positive and good impression when you meet people for the first time.

Keep reading to learn more about the habits or signs or traits of boring people and how can get over those things.

20 Signs of a Boring Person:

Boring people always do the same!

Boring people are always bored, restless, and unhappy

Boring people are hanging with the wrong crowd

Boring people are talking too much without adding value

Boring people are too focused on their problems

Boring people can't make anyone laugh

Boring people don't have anything interesting to say

Boring people don't have balanced conversations

Boring people don't have the ability to include others into the conversation

Boring people don't have the ability to take the perspective of another

Boring people don't have their own personality

Boring people don't know how to become a good storyteller

Boring people don't understand if others are engaged in their conversation

Boring people have poor improvisational skills

Boring people lose their sense of wonder and imagination

Boring people never put your phone down for a minute

Boring people repeat themselves when starting to talk

Boring people start talking in a monotone voice always

Boring people stuck inside their comfort zone

Boring people thoughts are constantly negative

How to Stop or Not to Be Boring Person:

1. Take Control Of The Conversation:

The key to becoming an interesting person and avoid boredom altogether is by taking control of the conversation. You should speak about things that interests people the most. However this could differ from group to group.

Speak about intelligent topics such as religion, politics, taboos, law etc. This will definitely help you make a good impression and save you from become a bore.

However, make sure you have researched carefully before speaking. You don't want to give away false information and get caught in the end.

Use your words carefully, refrain from speaking excessively and the rest will be taken care of.

2. Don't use phones in social gatherings:

You wouldn't come across as a very interesting person if you are constantly checking emails and text messages on your phone.

Yes, we all want to stay updated but when you are attending a party or an event, focus on the people you are surrounded with instead of getting stuck with your phone.

This will make you look like a less disrespectful and a more approachable person.

Not just that, speaking to people around you can also help in breaking the awkwardness and allowing people to have a chance to get to know you more.

3. Don't be shy:

Shy people are often considered boring and we are sure you want to avoid that if you want to come across as interesting and fun loving.

So remember to be more charismatic. Also remember this will be the last time you meet people around you. This will encourage you to be a more engaging and energetic person.

4. Stop wasting time on things that don't matter:

One of the best ways in which you could stop being boring is not to waste time altogether. Don't spend too much time on the internet or the television.

Not only does it occupy your brain but also takes over your mind. These things make you less carefree and stop you from being what you can actually become.

So in order to become less boring, stop doing any of those things that are way too time and effort consuming.

5. Don't wait for the perfect moment:

If you are someone who is hoping to speak to people when the time is right, then you are doing it absolutely wrong. It is never too good to wait for the best moment. The smartest thing you could do is maximize the time that you already have.

6. Learn to be attractive with the words you use:

When you're speaking to someone, you can learn to be a much more attractive person with the sort of words you are already using.

Make sure you ask questions that are important. Also when they are stating their ideas, show some interest in what they have to tell.

Not just that, you need to show that you are engaged in the conversation so don't forget to look into their eyes.

Smile a little when they say something nice. Lean forward gently and use facial expressions to show that you care.

7. Improve Body Language:

If you didn't know improving your body language can help you, you'll be surprised how much people are going to be attracted to you.

Everyone is going to love you and find you less boring because of how you react to their words. Always keep your toes pointed towards them.

Don't keep your hands crossed or akimbo. When they are saying something, tell them to keep going. This will help you get a better grasp of the conversation.

8. Work Some More On Your Fun Qualities:

When we advise you to improve on your fun qualities, we are basically hoping that you will learn to become a more confident person.

Before you try to become a fun person, you should tell yourself that you already are one. There is really nothing wrong in believing in loving and accepting yourself. Just know that you can do it and you definitely will.

Learn to leave the negative ideas behind and focus on the positive. Know that you aren't perfect and that you will never be.

Boost your self-esteem by making a list of your successes and failures and remind yourself to maximize your time and have more fun.

Do not be way too confident about yourself. Know that you are not perfect and everyone is bound to make mistakes. Try to be humble and love yourself.

9. Try to be open minded:

When you stop being narrow minded, life automatically becomes far more interesting. Here are some ways in which you can work on this quality!

Always be willing to try new things. It could be planned from beforehand. If you have a friend who loves to attend operas and you don't, go along with them anyway. It will help you learn something new and improve your friendship with them as well.

Also remember that everyone has a different opinion. You can still be best friends with people despite having disagreements or differing opinions on topics such as religion and politics. Always remember to look for the things you have in common. If you think your friend has some controversial opinions, then its best to avoid it altogether.

10. Smile, laugh and say a few jokes:

Smiling, laughing and cracking a few jokes will not just ease the tension but also stop you from being boring.

Even though you don't feel like smiling at times, you definitely should. This will let off a positive and friendly vibe about you.

However, don't overdo it or you will come across as an annoying person. And when it comes to cracking jokes, make sure you say something funny when the time is right.

Also don't do something you aren't comfortable with. Try something ridiculous like wearing a graphic tee with some silly messages on it. That should surely pull off the boring tag!

11. Always be ready to explore:

Always be ready to learn new things. Look out for new opportunities and build on new skills and techniques. Go and scour new places and tell your friends about it. Hang out together and have fun! There are some great ways in which you can improve that right away

Have a good idea about the area you live in. Know about the best restaurant and places here. People love to eat. So when you find a good place to dine, tell all your friends about it and be there. Look for outdoor corners and make suggestions too.

Always think outside the box. Learn a new skill if you can. Go read some poetry, learn some cooking, check out a couple of museums, cooking classes, yoga centre or even Zumba classes. Whenever there is an opportunity to participate at a concert, go ahead and do so. It will allow you to become a more interesting and enthusiastic person.

12. Know what's popular:

To grab attention and be less boring, you have to know what's popular. If you happen to have a solid base, you can definitely become the star of the group with your ability to indulge into various topics for conversation.

Also read the room carefully before you say something. Do not criticize way too much. Know your opinion and state in a decent manner. You don't want to turn anybody off.

Conclusion:

No matter what, make sure you are having fun in life. Because when you are enjoying, people around you will begin to enjoy as well. Always be honest and show how trustworthy and reliable you are.

Also respect people and treat them how they should be. Show some interest in them and they will definitely show some in you.

Make sure you hang out with people who are fun too. The point is to maximize your talents and make use of what you have. If you are a very reserved person, this could be a little difficult at first. But with a little effort, you can definitely improve.

The tips and ideas should definitely help you in the longer run. So here's hoping that you learn to change yourself and transform into a fun loving and enthusiastic individual very soon.

64 Things to Do When You're Bored

oredom can feel impossible to escape. This is particularly true now, when many of us are stuck indoors due to social-distancing efforts necessary to slow the spread of COVID-19. Some people have children keeping them busy; others have even more work during this crisis. Others are just inside, looking at the same walls they've been looking at for days, potentially alone, and feeling like nothing can pull them out of this funk.

Well, don't worry; boredom is a state of mind, and we want to break you out of it. Below, we've gathered up 60 great spirit-lifting, boredom-busting ideas to try next time you're feeling spiritless and bored. Good luck and have fun.

Entertaining Things

1. Start watching a new reality series. Maybe you want to finally get into Top Chef, or maybe you've never watched a single episode of Real Housewives? Reality shows are designed to keep you watching, which can be a boon for a bored brain.
2. Watch a classic movie you've never seen. It's time to finally check out what Casablanca is all about.
3. Read a great essay. You don't have to look too far.
4. Search "happy birthday + [your name]" on YouTube. It doesn't technically have to be your birthday to enjoy watching a bunch of strangers sing to you.
5. Make a playlist of your favorite songs from high school. I bet you haven't heard Eve 6's "Inside Out" in a long time, have you? What about Jimmie's Chicken Shack "Do Right"?
6. Watch as many episodes as you want of your favorite show. Listen, who cares. Just keep watching it until it stops being fun.
7. Start a book you've been meaning to read. It's time to finally check out what (at least the beginning of) Swann's Way is all about.
8. Play a video game. If you're without a video game system, there are tons of free options online.
9. Read some humor writing. Delight your mind with the writings of Jack Handey, or Samantha Irby.
10. Put together a puzzle. If you enjoy that sort of thing.
11. Make a music video playlist to play on your TV. This is almost like being at a bar, sort of.

Relaxing Things

12. Perform turn-down service for yourself. Before you go to bed, why not prepare your room as if you're in a hotel?
13. Give yourself a manicure and pedicure. An at-home salon-worthy manicure is possible, trust us.
14. Apply a soothing face mask. Your skin deserves it.
15. Do a guided meditation. Maybe this one by Puff Daddy?
16. Have a yoga break. There are a bunch of great, free yoga classes you can take online. It'll feel good, whether it's a 15 minute or hour-long session.
17. Take a bath. Do you have a nice bathtub? Please, appreciate your great fortune, get in it, and take a bath.
18. Go for a walk. It's still allowed, and it can do wonders for your mindset.
19. Practice deep breathing. I know it might sound like it won't do much,

but slowing down and paying attention to your breath can really change how you feel, both mentally and physically.

20. Lie down, close your eyes, and listen to a podcast. Even if you don't like podcasts, I bet this sounds pretty relaxing. Find an episode that sounds interesting, lie down, and listen.

21. Cuddle with your pet. It's good for both you and your pet!

22. Take an online museum tour. There are lots of choices these days!

Delicious Things

23. Make a fancy cocktail or mocktail. Practice your mixology skills and make yourself a beautiful drink.

24. Find your ingredients and Google them. Sometimes you're looking around your kitchen thinking, "I have ingredients, but I'm not sure if they go together?" The easiest thing to do is input them all into Google and see what recipes the search engine suggests. Red pepper lemon pasta, maybe?

25. Bake bread. Just give into it.

26. Meal prep for the week. It can be very satisfying! (Though you should consider whether getting all of your meal prep done now will take away future boredom-busting cooking opportunities.)

27. Bake cookies. Mmm. Wouldn't cookies be good right now?

28. Try to re-create your favorite restaurant meal. You don't need to be a chef, all you need to be is a person with the appropriate ingredients and a lot of derring-do.

29. Make a dip. Oh, gosh. What is your favorite dip? Onion dip? Guacamole? Artichoke? The nice thing about making a dip for yourself is you end up with a lot of dip. All for you!

30. Plan your breakfast for tomorrow. Maybe some overnight oats?

31. Make homemade peeps. Or, on second thought, maybe don't.

32. Soak some dry beans. Then, later, you can have some beans.

33. Make applesauce. It's seriously so easy.

Creative Things

34. Paint a portrait of your cat. Or your dog, or your rabbit, or your bookshelf! Then you get a bonus activity: choosing where to display it.

35. Write a song. Do you have a musical instrument around? It might be time to dust it off and write a song about whatever it is you're feeling right now.

36. Start a journal. Don't you wish you had always journaled, so you could go back and read about how your life was five, ten, or fifteen years ago? Well, it's not too late to start. In five, ten, or fifteen years, you'll be glad you did.

37. Teach your dog a new trick. Teach your dog to spin, or give her paw, or "play dead." It's a fun and rewarding activity for both of you.
38. Learn a dance. Maybe something from TikTok, or something from one of your favorite music videos.
39. Write a poem. No one ever has to read it.
40. Learn how to juggle. Can you imagine how impressed your friends will be once you reveal that you've taught yourself how to juggle?
41. Write letters. As a kid, there was absolutely nothing more exciting than the idea of getting a letter in the mail from a pen pal. Why do we let time change us? Why do we let age rob us of our youthful sense of wonder? Send a letter to a friend. Maybe they'll write back!
42. Start a photo and memories album. If you're like me, you keep a lot of little pieces of trash around, for memories. Movie stubs, playbills, particularly notable receipts. Why not gather up all this garbage into a photo album? You can even also include photos.
43. Turn a T-shirt into a sleeveless shirt. Do you have a T-shirt you like but never wear, maybe because it doesn't look good, or isn't the right size? Maybe it will be a little better if you cut off the sleeves.
44. Read a play, or write one. It's like watching a movie, except it's reading (or writing).
45. Sew a mask for a friend. An act of love and of creativity.
46. Design your future tattoo. Are you thinking about getting a tattoo? Why not one that you've designed? Draw some stuff, play around, imagine where it could be inked permanently into your flesh.
47. Learn how to read tarot cards. Here's an easy beginner's guide.
48. Learn about bog bodies. You're going to be surprised.
49. Make a Covid time capsule. Maybe someday you'll want to remember this?

Productive Things

50. Deep clean your bathroom. When you're bored, it can be helpful to just discard the idea that you're going to find something "fun" to do, and get down to some work that actually needs doing. First, I'm sure your bathroom needs a good scrubbing. Why not do it now?
51. Organize your closet. Having an organized space helps you know what you have, and it helps you find things, and it helps you feel relaxed. Go ahead and organize that closet.
52. Clean out your fridge. Something smells in there.
53. Start learning a new language. Does Duolingo even work? I don't know,

but you can try.
54. Wash the windows. They're looking pretty grimy. Let the sunshine in!
55. Hand-wash your clothes. A nice thing to check off of the to-do list.
56. Do an online workout. It's so nice to have done a workout. Unfortunately, the only way to have done a workout is to do a workout. So go on and get that serotonin.
57. Clean your makeup brushes. Trust us, they're disgusting.
58. Organize all those papers. You know you have a big stack of papers. Or maybe you have a few little stacks of papers. What are all of those papers? Bills? Or something else? Time to organize them.
59. Clean your window-unit air conditioner. Ugh, God, this is going to be so annoying but you do have to do it, so. Maybe just do it now.
60. Swap out your candles. If you keep a lot of scented candles in your home, chances are you store them seasonally, bringing out spring candles during the spring, winter candles during the winter, etc. Maybe it's time to swap for the next season?
61. Clean out your computer's hard drive. There are no doubt tons of files clogging up your computer that you downloaded a long time ago and have absolutely no use for. Delete them and free up some space for more stuff you don't need later.
62. Wash the floors. Oh gosh, wouldn't it be nice to have clean floors?
63. Rotate your mattress. I personally have never done this. But maybe we both should?
64. Organize your pantry. Ahh, can you imagine it? An organized pantry, where you can see everything you have and grab whatever you need. Does it seem like an impossible dream? It's not.

World's most boring man: 'Weird' way 3 million people are falling asleep

Drew Ackerman is possibly the world's most boring man.

The 45-year-old from California is so boring, in fact, people who listen to his podcast are tipped into a state of total unconsciousness, usually within minutes of hearing his nonsensical, monotonous rambling.

In Australia alone, more than 150,000 people listen to him each night before we shut our eyes.

This may sound like a complete turn-off to the average person who prefers to be awake and entertained by their choice of podcast, but

Ackerman says his approach is saving millions of lives around the world.

His podcast, Sleep With Me, allows more than three million people each month living with insomnia and anxiety to drift into a deep, peaceful slumber.

So how has one man developed the power to put this many people to sleep each night?

DESPERATELY SEEKING SLEEP

Ackerman's troubled relationship with sleep began many years before the 2013 launch of Sleep With Me.

As a boy he suffered from insomnia and anxiety for years and would often get "so stressed I'd lie awake at night worrying, over-thinking things".

Many years later, he found a routine that helped him wind down before bed, but he couldn't find any podcasts available that weren't structured or regimented sleep meditations.

"There was nothing that was similar to a children's bedtime story for adults to fall asleep to," Ackerman said.

Ackerman, who worked as a librarian at the time, designed Sleep With Me to feel as if the listener was having an "easy conversation with your friend from across the room".

"I knew the pain and loneliness of not being able to fall asleep, and the idea of having someone there to keep you company as you fall asleep is really comforting," he said.

And so, the very first hour-long episode of Sleep With Me was recorded.

Admittedly, it took Ackerman at least 150 episodes before he truly understood what it took to be the most boring person on earth.

Even now, he finds himself falling asleep to the sound of his own voice while editing over lunch.

"Yep, I have fallen asleep to my own podcast before," he laughed.

Now with 785 episodes in his bedtime arsenal, Ackerman's twice-weekly podcast features him meandering slowly through an unpredictable 60 minutes, filled to bursting with "intentionally boring content" — all delivered in his trademark slow, continuous pace.

His trademark tone is even and calm, with listeners claiming their snoozing in mere minutes after listening to his nonsensical tales.

Why has he done this for so long? Because of the "humbling" feedback he gets from his millions of fans around the world.

"When I hear what listeners have been through and how I have helped, it's a huge moment for me," he said.

"It might be a soldier dealing with PTSD or a new mum trying to take care of her baby or someone working a second or third shift who is trying to get some sleep during the day."

WHAT'S IN AN EPISODE?

Ackerman describes his bedtime stories as ramblings "that don't really make any particular sense".

"Sometimes I go on journeys, where I personify landmarks and have discussions with them," he said.

In one episode, Ackerman pretends he is interviewing the iconic Sydney Harbour Bridge.

"People can picture that in their head, and I then personify that bridge," he said.

"I tend to overdo it on the detail and try to talk to the bridge, asking it, 'What does it feel like to be looked at, looked through and looked from?'

"The listeners are usually like, 'What is this guy going on about, but by then they're asleep'."

His secret is to keep his stories interesting enough to keep you listening without stimulating your brain.

While Ackerman admits his entire podcast "is always pretty weird", the most unusual episode he ever recorded was a confronting interview with his imaginary friend from childhood — Bill.

"I had to call my mum before the episode to ask her what his name was because I had totally forgotten it. His name was Bill," Ackerman said.

For the next 60 minutes, Ackerman spoke to Bill about his life, asked him questions about what he had been up to and even apologised for forgetting about him.

"I had to apologise to Bill so I told him, "I forgot all about you and I'm really sorry'. People liked it," he said.

WHAT HELPS US FALL ASLEEP?

For Ackerman, the interactive nature of Sleep With Me allows him to gauge what people like to listen to before they drift off.

He said there were a number of things his listeners hated hearing before they dozed off.

"They don't like me talking about snakes and spiders or air travel or flying of any kind," he said.

"They also don't want to hear about financial problems or politics."

But his insomniacs love being immersed in a tactile experience or a tour of something they can picture in their mind's eye.

FAN BASE

Ackerman has a strong following in Australia — racking up 150,000 downloads across the nation each month.

"There's fans all over the world like the UAE, Iceland and even Africa, where English is their second or third language," he said.

"There is this massive population of people struggling in every country to get a decent night's sleep, and I want to help them."

But people could require Ackerman's bizarre stream of consciousness more than they realise.

Based on a national survey, it is estimated that 13 per cent of New Zealanders aged 20–59 yrs suffer from symptoms of insomnia.

To help his Aussie audience, Ackerman released a one-off Australian-inspired sleep episode this week that features him meandering through some of the nation's greatest landmarks, from the Big Banana to the Sydney Harbour Bridge.

He produced the episode in partnership with natural sleep supplement company, Floris ReDromin Forte.

According to Ackerman, the episode, called "Australia Sleepy Slang Tour" is a silly, lighthearted walk around the country.

"We decided that I would go on a tour of Australian landmarks, ask for sleep tips from those landmarks and learn some Aussie slang," Ackerman said.

"My pronunciation was terrible, and all the landmarks were having fun at my expense."

Ways to Combat Boredom in a Relationship

The harsh reality of long term relationships: Boredom hits.

As time goes by and the relationship's honeymoon phase recedes further and further in the rearview mirror, it's likely that the exciting chemistry you and your partner once had just isn't as present anymore. You might find yourself on autopilot, in a monotonous routine with your partner, and next thing you know, you're straight up bored.

When a relationship is newer, there tends to be more excitement. You're experiencing a lot of firsts with your partner, sparks are flying, and you're having fun. When a relationship is older, it's common to experience boredom in some aspect of your relationship, whether it's your day-to-day life at home with your partner, your lack of date nights, your sex life, or all of the above.

Should You Be Concerned About Boredom In A Relationship?

If you're bored in your current relationship, you definitely aren't alone. Talkspace therapist Cynthia Catchings, LCSW- S, explains, "Boredom is normal. We cannot be happy and celebrating all the time. In the same way, we cannot be active and enjoying every moment with our partner."

Since this is something that's pretty normal, you might be wondering if you should be concerned if you're experiencing a lackluster phase. Luckily, boredom in a relationship isn't necessarily a glaring red flag. Being bored doesn't automatically mean that you're with the wrong partner or that the relationship is doomed and destined to fail.

Being comfortable versus being bored

Take a step back and have a good look at your relationship. Ask yourself this: Are you confusing being comfortable with being bored? Or is the fact that you're feeling comfortable making you bored? Are you simply missing the way sparks used to fly? Try to pinpoint any specifics that go along with your boredom. What aspects of the relationship are you bored with? Identifying what you don't like about the current state of your relationship is the first step to changing it.

Ask yourself: Do you want to fix it?

While boredom itself isn't a red flag, you should be concerned if neither of you really care about doing something to "fix" it. Catchings says, "If we know boredom has knocked on our door, both partners should communicate and create ways to bring back the sparkle." She adds, "Lack of interest in doing so could indicate that the relationship might be in trouble. At this stage it is important to evaluate the thoughts and behaviors we have towards our partner and the relationship as a whole."

Oh, and a boring sex life should be something you want to work on doing something about, too. Studies have linked infidelity to sexual boredom; The Normal Bar, the largest scale survey on relationships out there, found that for people who cheated on their partners, boredom was the reason that 71% of men and 49% of women gave in to infidelity.

Ideas To Spruce Things Up

There are definitely ways to beat boredom in a relationship — and they don't necessarily include spending lots of money or jetting off to somewhere exotic. Simple ways to spruce things up certainly exist. Just because you aren't experiencing many typical relationship firsts anymore doesn't mean you can't try new things together. In fact, it's all the more reason to get spontaneous. Even doing little things that deviate from your norm can create new couples' firsts, fresh memories, and most importantly, excitement!

Up the adrenaline and try something adventurous, like taking a surf lesson or trying a new kind of fitness class together. Doing something that's fresh and gets your heart rate up can ignite a spark and take you back to the times where you and your partner first got each other all worked up. Or, put a new focus on doing a bunch of little things and enjoying the simple pleasures in a different light.

Here are a few easy ideas Catching suggests for couples dealing with boredom:

Have a "day/night out" every week

Be creative and decorate a room together

Prepare a nice dinner at home

Make a gift for your partner

Enjoy each other's company with a glass of wine or iced tea

Leave Post-Its around the house telling your partner you love him/her/them

Get a babysitter or family friend to take care of the children and go for a walk or to the movies

Cuddle on the couch and watch your favorite show or movie — popcorn is a plus!

Send lunch to your partner's office with a nice note

Escape for a weekend to a local or even a more distant B&B

Breakfast in bed with a loving note

Boredom with your sex life is a whole other aspect, albeit one that can be fixed with some communication, effort, and an open mind. Be honest and straightforward with each other, even though it can definitely be awkward at the beginning.

Here are some tips for combating sexual boredom:

Tell your partner your biggest turn ons, and ask them to share their biggest turn ons with you

Share your fantasies with each other

Watch porn together to get some new ideas

Send a sexy text or photo to build up some excitement and anticipation

Ask for what you want in bed

Have a change of scenery (if you only have sex in the bedroom, try the shower, the living room, or the kitchen counter...bonus points for originality)

Try out role playing

Switch up who instigates the sex session

Getting a Professional Involved

Unfortunately, it is possible that your efforts might not work as well as you'd hoped. In this case, it might be time to bring in a professional — and that's absolutely nothing to be ashamed of.

Catchings says, "Look for a counselor that specializes in couples. Many couples reject the idea or wait too long to do this and when they feel the boat is sinking they want to start the therapy process." She adds, "Prevention is key and having a professional guiding you, with their expertise and care, could be the best investment you could ever make to save your relationship."

Ultimately, to get through this rough patch in the relationship, you're going to have to put in effort. You can't fight boredom with inaction. You'll have to work to bring some spark and fun back into your relationship, but it'll be so worth it.

Talkspace articles are written by experienced mental health-wellness contributors; they are grounded in scientific research and evidence-based practices. Articles are extensively reviewed by our team of clinical experts (therapists and psychiatrists of various specialties) to ensure content is accurate and on par with current industry standards.

Our goal at Talkspace is to provide the most up-to-date, valuable, and objective information on mental health-related topics in order to help readers make informed decisions.

Articles contain trusted third-party sources that are either directly linked to in the text or listed at the bottom to take readers directly to the source.

The 40 Most Boring Jobs in the World (Apparently).

Not too long ago, depressingly, we had someone leave the business.

Someone we didn't actually want to lose.

When we asked why they were leaving, they said they'd become 'bored' in their job.

— Cue lots of introspection about what we doing to make someone feel that way, and how we could put it right.

But what it also did was get us thinking about how we could put an end to workplace boredom for good, from both an employer's and employee's perspective.

And we're not just talking about having to do the odd tedious little task. Everyone has to do that.

We're talking full-on, mind-numbing boredom that crushes your soul.

Which gave us a little blog idea...

We mused over what we thought might be the most boring jobs in the world. The kind of mundane job you'd do anything to get out of.

So we did a little digging (it's amazing what you can find on the web!)

And it would seem that these 40 jobs fit into that description... what do you think?

The 40 Most Boring Jobs in the World (Apparently)

1. Frozen Pea Tester.

The person who tests the temperature of frozen peas on a production line.

2. Bookmark String Threader.

The person who threads the string through the end of a bookmark.

3. Printer Paper Feeder.

The person who sits in the printer room and refills the paper trays when they run out or jam.

4. Lift Operator.

The person who opens the lift, greets you and presses the buttons for you.

5. Milk Bottle Squeezer.

The person who squeezes all the milk bottles to make sure they're not leaking.

6. Pork Scratching Spotter.

The person who makes sure no hairy pork scratchings make it into the packet.

7. Cheese Slicer.

The person who slices up the cheese before it gets packaged.

8. Bitumen Tester.

The person who tests the viscosity of the bitumen.

9. Tablet Picker.

The person who picks the broken tablets out before packaged.

10. Label Sticker.

The person who sticks labels on boxes and envelopes.

11. Fax Operator.

The person who sits to watch and make sure the fax machines don't over-heat.

12. Stapler.

The person who staples all the documentation.

13. Un-stapler

And the person who un-staples all of it.

14. Box Packer.

The person who packs boxes.

15. Almond Grader.

The person who loads almonds into a machine so they can be separated by size and packaged.

16. Beetroot Pickling Line Cleaner.

The person who has to clean up the rotten beetroot bits off the floor, when they've been picked out from the production line.

17. Washing Powder Weigher.

The person who had to make sure 500g of washing powder goes into the box.

18. Night Security Guard.

The person who has to stay awake all night in an empty factory, in the middle of nowhere.

19. Envelope Stuffer.

The person who stuffs hundreds of envelopes a day.

20. Envelope Sticker (or Licker).

The person who closes the envelopes, once stuffed.

21. Post Opener.

The person who filters through the post, opening each and every piece.

22. Trophy Polisher.

The person who polishes trophies, all day.

23. Tour Guide Operator.

The person that does the same tour, at the same time, every day.

24. Step Attendant.

The person who stands by the step and warns you to "mind the step."

25. Sign Holder/ Human Sign.

The person that holds or is dressed as a sign with directions to a restaurant, take away or event.

26. Sausage Flipper.

The person that flips sausages on a production line.

27. Disney World Ride Attendant.

The person that has to say the same (scripted) greeting to everyone as they get on the ride.

28. Toll Booth Operator.

The person who collects cash at the toll.

29. Box Maker.

The person who makes hundreds of boxes, from templates every day.

30. Paper Counter.

The person who must count 50 reams of paper, and put them in separate packages.

31. Soil Infiltration Tester.

The person who watches water infiltrating soil through a pipe – measuring how much sinks each hour.

32. Waking Night.

The person who has to stay awake in a dark, warm room all night in a hospital.

33.Car Park Ticket Dispenser.

The person who has to manually let people out of the carpark, because the ticket machine is broken or too far away for people to reach.

34. Canal Guard.

The person who has to hang around the canal, in case anyone falls in.

35. Manual Un-subscriber.

The person who had to manually unsubscribe thousands of people from a mailing list.

36. Paint Watcher.

The person who literally has to watch paint dry.

37. Questionnaire Coder.

The person who has to write big numbers next to answers on a completed questionnaire, so it's easier and faster for data inputters to input into their computer.

38. Scanned Documents Typist.

The person who has to type up old and scanned documents.

39. The Fire Checker.

The person who has to walk around an old building, to make sure it's not on fire.

40. Social Media "Likers."

The person who likes your Facebook page etc. to make you look more popular.

I know what you're thinking; have I made some of these up? Well, I wish I had!

These are the weirdest and most wonderful boring jobs I could find across the web (surely they should be automated?!)

Of course, one man's meat is another man's poison – and to a certain extent a job is what you make of it.

Never a dull moment

Things get interesting when psychologists take a closer look at boredom.

Videos of fish-farm management techniques or men silently hanging laundry probably don't top your Netflix queue. And that's the point. These are some of the tedium-inducing tools that psychologists are using to study boredom in the lab.

"Even though boredom is very common, there is a lack of knowledge about it," says Wijnand van Tilburg, a psychologist at the University of Southampton. "There hasn't been much research about how it affects people on an everyday basis."

Now that's changing, as scientists have begun to take a closer look at this underappreciated emotion. The results of their research are anything but dull.

Boredom is a universal experience, yet until recently researchers didn't have a go-to definition of the condition. Psychologist John Eastwood, PhD, of York University in Toronto, decided that was a good place to start. He and his colleagues scoured the scientific literature for theories of boredom and tried to extract the common elements. Then they interviewed hundreds of people about what it feels like to experience that tedious state.

They concluded that boredom is best described in terms of attention. A bored person doesn't just have nothing to do. He or she wants to be stimulated, but is unable, for whatever reason, to connect with his or her environment — a state Eastwood describes as an "unengaged mind" (Perspectives on Psychological Science, 2012).

"In a nutshell, it boiled down to boredom being the unfulfilled desire for satisfying activity," he says.

From listless to focused

One of the more surprising aspects of Eastwood's definition is that boredom can be associated with both low-arousal and high-arousal states. At times, boredom breeds lethargy — you might even have trouble keeping your eyes open. In other situations, being bored can lead to an agitated restlessness: think pacing, or constantly tapping your feet. Often, he says, boredom oscillates between the two states. You might pump yourself up to concentrate on a dreary task, then slip back into listlessness as your focus wavers again.

Some of us are more likely than others to suffer the effects of an unengaged mind. Unsurprisingly, given boredom's close connection with attention, people with chronic attention problems such as attention-deficit hyperactivity disorder have a high propensity for ennui. James Danckert, PhD, a professor of cognitive neuroscience at the University of Waterloo, found that people highly prone to boredom perform poorly on tasks that require sustained attention, and are more likely to show increased symptoms of both ADHD and depression (Experimental Brain Research, 2012).

Chronic boredom can look a lot like depression, but "they're not the same emotional experience," Danckert says. Together with Eastwood and other colleagues, he surveyed more than 800 people and found that boredom and depression were highly correlated, but were distinct states (Journal of Social and Clinical Psychology, 2011).

More work needs to be done to understand the relationship between these experiences, says Eastwood, but he speculates that boredom may be a risk factor for depression. "When people are bored, they're disengaged from satisfying activity and more likely to become internally focused in a negative, ruminative cycle," he says.

People with a high sensitivity to reward are also at risk of boredom. These sensation seekers — such as the skydivers among us — are particularly likely to find the world moves too slowly. At the opposite end of the spectrum, people who are overly sensitive to pain and punishment — such as people with high anxiety — are more likely to withdraw from the world out of self-protection. They may end up understimulated as a result.

Eastwood has also found that people with alexithymia, a condition marked by an inability to identify and describe one's own emotions, are more prone to boredom (Personality and Individual Differences, 2007). "Feelings are like compass points that help orient us," he says. "If we lack emotional awareness, we lack the capacity to select appropriate targets for engagement with the world."

Killer doldrums

In many ways, boredom is a modern luxury. Danckert says, the word "boring" as it's used now didn't even enter common parlance until the industrial revolution gave us time to spare. "Early on in human history, when our ancestors had to spend most of their days securing food and shelter, boredom wasn't an option," he says.

In today's electronic world, it's rare to be stuck with absolutely nothing to do. Most of us are bombarded by near-constant stimuli such as tweets, texts and a seemingly limitless supply of cat videos right at our fingertips. But all those diversions don't seem to have alleviated society's collective boredom. The reverse may be true, says Eastwood.

"These might distract you in the short run, but I think it makes you more susceptible to boredom in the long run, and less able to find ways to engage yourself," he says.

Teresa Belton, PhD, a research associate in the school of education and lifelong learning at the University of East Anglia, agrees. In 2001, she studied the influence of television on children's storytelling. She found the main ingredient in children's stories was their own direct experience. She attributed some of the lack of imagination in many stories to children's resorting to TV time when they were bored (Media, Culture and Society, 2001). Given the steep rise in the use of technology since then, she suggests the tendency to alleviate boredom with screen time may have become even more prevalent.

"Whenever children are bored, they're likely to turn on one of these electronic things and be bombarded with stimuli from the external world rather than having to rely on internal resources or devise their own activities," Belton says.

Even without a smartphone, tedium is usually temporary. Eventually you reach the front of the line at the DMV, and even the dullest academic lecture draws to a close.

Danckert became interested in boredom while studying patients with severe brain injuries. "When I ask traumatic brain injury patients if they're more bored post-injury, they all say yes," he says, adding that chronic dissatisfaction with the world can lead them to engage in risky and impulsive behaviors.

Being underwhelmed can be problematic for the rest of us as well. It's correlated with drug abuse, gambling and overeating. Eastwood is studying how tedium affects gambling behavior in the lab. The research is preliminary, he says, but so far it appears that men are more likely to make risky bets when they're bored.

There's even evidence that the phrase "bored to death" has some truth to it. As part of the Whitehall II Study, begun in 1985, British civil servants answered questions about social determinants of health, including some questions about boredom. More than two decades later, Annie Britton, PhD, and Martin Shipley, PhD, compared their responses with death records. They found the people who reported experiencing a great deal of boredom were more likely to die young than those who were more engaged with the world (International Journal of Epidemiology, 2010). The researchers theorize that boredom was probably a proxy for other risk factors, such as drug and alcohol use. Boredom is also associated with performance detriments, which in some cases can lead to serious problems.

"We know when people are bored they're more likely to make performance errors and likely to not be as productive," says Eastwood. "That's a big deal if you're an air-traffic controller or you're monitoring a nuclear plant."

On the other hand, boredom can prompt people to move out of tedious routines. Belton recently interviewed people known for their creative success, including an artist, a novelist, a poet and a neuroscientist. "They all said boredom can instigate new thinking and prod them into trying new things," she says.

The poet took up his craft in middle age after finding himself stuck in a hospital bed for several hours with nothing to do. The only paper he had available was a stack of Post-It Notes, so he began writing poetry, the most practical activity to fit on three square inches.

"If people don't have the inner resources to deal with boredom constructively, they might do something destructive to fill the void," Belton says. "Those who have the patience to stay with that feeling, and the imagination and confidence to try out new ideas, are likely to make something creative out of it."

Looking for meaning

Psychologists' research has also begun to hint at the ways boredom can affect behavior, for better or worse. In a study done while he was at the University of Limerick, Van Tilburg and colleagues made participants' eyes glaze over by asking them to copy dull literature references and make repetitive drawings. A control group did the same, but for a much shorter period of time. Afterward the researchers cued participants to retrieve memories. They found the highly bored people called up more nostalgic memories (Emotion, 2012).

"Feelings of nostalgia are associated with seeing your life in a broader perspective," says Van Tilburg. "We saw that boredom actually increased people's tendency to recall these very nostalgic memories and actually made them feel that life in general was more meaningful."

In another study, Van Tilburg showed Irish study participants images of clovers and lists of traditional Irish names. When the participants were bored using the same techniques in the previous study, they responded more positively to these symbols of their national identity. But they were also more antagonistic toward members of an out-group. When asked to recommend a jail sentence for a hypothetical criminal, the bored subjects were harsher than the non-bored when sentencing a perpetrator said to be of English rather than Irish heritage (Personality and Social Psychology Bulletin, 2011).

What that means, Van Tilburg says, is that when people are unengaged, they seek meaning wherever they can — whether that's with a fond recollection from the past or a misguided sense of patriotism.

"Boredom signals what you're doing right now seems to be lacking purpose," he explains. "As soon as you offer people alternative behaviors that may give them a sense of purpose, they're more eager to engage, and this can result in negative or positive behavior."

Van Tilburg's findings could have implications for dealing with boredom in constructive ways. "You can imagine situations like nursing homes, where it might be difficult for the elderly to find activities that alleviate boredom," he says.

Other researchers are also investigating ways to alleviate monotony, especially in the classroom. Ulrike Nett, PhD, at the University of Konstanz, Germany, and colleagues compared strategies that high school students used to cope with boredom in math class. Some took a cognitive approach, such as reminding themselves how learning math would help them reach their career goals. Others used an avoidance strategy, such as chatting with friends. As it turned out, the students who took the cognitive approach experienced less boredom than the avoiders (Contemporary Educational Psychology (PDF, 622KB), 2011).

Despite these promising starts, don't expect scientists to cure ennui just yet. "If there hasn't been much research done on causes and consequences of boredom," Eastwood says, "there's been even less done on coping with it."

7 Ways to Make Small Talk Way More Interesting

Stop boring yourself -- and others -- silly at events

There are few pleasures in life better than a great conversation. When you truly connect with someone, time stands still, space contracts, and you leave whatever event you were at feeling truly alive.

On the other hand, there are few miseries worse than a night of endless small talk. An evening of surreptitious glances at the bar and awkward silences will leave you as drained and depressed as a night of new friendships will leave you exhilarated.

So how do you turn one into the other, moving from small talk drudgery to genuine human connection? You get better at small talk, obviously -- or to be more accurate you learn how to get beyond small talk and into the realm of real conversation. Quora can help.

The question-and-answer site crowdsourced wisdom for a user who wanted to know how to get better at small talk, gathering useful tips for anyone who wants to grow their circle of connections and make their next event way less boring (for all involved).

1. Be more interested.

If you want small talk to be more interesting, the surest route is to be more interested in your conversation partner. "If you are running out of things to say, you are not interested enough in the person you are talking with," insists angel investor Kai Peter Chang in the thread's most popular answer.

"If you don't fundamentally care about the person you are speaking with, that will show," he writes. "So the first fix is your own attitude -- if this is someone you don't care about that you are simply pretending to care about, cut your losses, say 'it's nice to meet you' (yes, lie) and move on."

Writer Ellen Vrana offers some advice: "Imagine a robot saying 'I find you interesting.' Creepy. Words alone don't work. To convey a genuine sense of interest, you have to emote. Lean forward. Make eye contact. Show them that you are listening and care."

2. Ask open-ended questions.

There's absolutely no trick that can make one-word answers exciting, so the only solution is to avoid them. It's all about phrasing, insists art director Craig Weiland. "When you ask someone a small-talky question, be aware of how the question is phrased, and always defer to open-ended structure in your phrasing of questions rather than ones with a simple yes or no answer," he advises.

"For example, 'Are you here with your family?' is a question that can be answered with a simple 'yes' and then you're left holding the bag again...

'Whom are you here with?' invites them to share new information of their own, introducing new subjects of conversation to discuss. If they reply, 'My family,' then you can ask about them, since the other party brought them into this themselves," he elaborates.

"Get out of small talk phase by asking simple questions that require more than one word 'yes/no' answers and pay attention to the responses," writes entrepreneur Daniel Da Vinci, concurring with both points one and two in a single sentence.

3. Leverage your environment (or your wardrobe).

Talking about the weather or the traffic is the classic example of this strategy, but there are other, less painfully cliched ways to use your environment as a conversational springboard. Software engineer Robert Rapplean suggests "commenting on something in your environment... their clothing or jewelry," for example.

It's a technique that's endorsed beyond Quora as well. On HBR recently, professional speaker (and therefore serial event attendee) Dorie Clark suggested a variation on this theme.

"Wearing a distinctive clothing item can be a great icebreaker, whether it's a Madeleine Albright-style signature brooch (which can spark a conversation about the trip to Italy where you bought it), a tie from your alma mater ('you're a Longhorn, too?!?'), or colorful socks," she writes, adding, that "you can also let your conversations be guided by someone else's sartorial choices. Psychologist Richard Wiseman wrote about one man with a unique networking strategy; to avoid habitually gravitating to people just like him, he would pick a color in advance and then make a point of seeking out people wearing that color to initiate conversations and make connections he otherwise wouldn't."

4. Play the student.

Small talk can seem pointless and unstructured -- and therefore totally painful -- but most everyone understands both the how and why of teaching. So one trick is to turn an aimless chat into a learning session.

"If there's a subject you're not familiar with, just be honest with that person and 9 out of 10 times they'll teach you about it," says entrepreneur Michael Wong. "It helps if you show a healthy interest though and put effort into following what's being said."

5. Gamify for your own amusement.

Boredom is usually a two-way street. If your conversation partner is bored, so are you. But the opposite is also true. If you're having a blast, it's likely others will enjoy talking to you. So "gamify for your own amusement," suggests social cause marketer Keirsten Lindholm. Before entering an event, she chooses a topic to find out more about and then uses small talk as an opportunity to complete her self-appointed mission.

"Sometimes I feel like finding out about secret hobbies, favorite volunteer activities or how their industry is changing," she says, adding that "trading ideas is like weaving a story together of playful banter and should probably be regarded as foreplay to possibility. The possibility of more time with one another."

6. Be more interesting.

If the first principle of good conversation is to be genuinely interested, an important corollary is to be more interesting. Small talk is only as small as your reservoir of topics and experiences. Expand your store of anecdotes and opinions and you'll expand your conversational possibilities.

"Get out there and experience new things!" urges respondent Belinda Kwan. "You need to build your repertoire of interesting experiences (not only for the sake of having good conversations, but for the sake of enjoying your life)." Good advice on the topic exists if you're not sure about how to go about becoming more interesting.

7. Give up on lost causes.

Finally, don't forget that you're not required to find every human being on the planet interesting (it would be weird if you did). The best thing you can do sometimes is cut your losses and end a stalled conversation in order to move on and chat with someone with whom you have more rapport.

"There are a few people who are as dull as toast. No, that's an insult to toast. Dull as a toaster that doesn't have toast. You won't connect with everyone. No one does," Vrana reassures readers of the thread.

CHAPTER EIGHT

How to Talk to a Girl Without It Getting Boring

The last time you talked to a girl, you found yourself rambling on about your math homework, then mentioning your dentist appointment, and concluding by cracking your knuckles while the girl stared at the floor in awkward silence. Don't fret: every guy has been there. It's okay if your last conversation wasn't exactly as exciting as the Hunger Games series -- if you're prepared and make an effort, then the next time you talk to a girl, she'll be utterly captivated.

Starting Off on the Right Foot

1

Start with a light topic. When you first start talking to the girl, pick a light topic that you can both chat about pretty casually that won't make things awkward. Don't tell her about the weird rash on your back or ask her about her most embarrassing moment; you can save that stuff for when you get to know each other better. Stick to the PG topics that can still lead to an interesting conversation without making the girl feel uncomfortable. Don't use profanity. She likes to be treated like a lady! Here are some pretty safe but fun topics that you can start off with:

Your favorite bands

Movies you've seen recently

Your pets

Your siblings

What you did over the weekend or what you're going to do next weekend

Your plans for the upcoming vacation

#THEGREENCHAIN IS A GLOBAL INITIATIVE DEDICATED TO DEVELOPING RENEWABLE ENERGY PROJECTS AND...

2

Avoid the personal stuff. Avoiding the personal stuff goes hand in hand with starting with a light topic. Though you can have a deeper discussion once the girl gets to know you better, for now, it's best to avoid talking about any deaths in the family, your first loves, your weird illnesses, or your fear of death. If you feel like you have an instant connection with the girl, then you really might be able to wade through the small talk faster to get to the important stuff, but you should still avoid highly personal topics when you just start talking or the girl may back off.

Okay, if she introduces a personal topic and is game for talking about it, then you can pursue it and see where it goes, but still try to stay on your toes.

Check out the girl's facial expressions and body language. If she backs away or looks upset when you ask her something that you thought was pretty simple, then she might actually view it as a sensitive topic

Keep smiling. Maintaining a smile and a positive demeanor will keep the girl's interest and will make her more likely to keep talking to you. Though you don't have to grin until your cheeks are numb, you should smile whenever it's appropriate. This will let the girl see that you really like talking to her and will leave her with a positive feeling. You may be so nervous that you forget to smile, so remember to keep yourself in check.[1]

Smiling is especially important when you first start talking to the girl and at the end of the conversation. It's important to start off and to finish strong.

Make eye contact. Making eye contact is key for making the girl feel important and like you really care about what she has to say. You may feel shy about talking to her and could end up staring at your feet or looking around just because you're afraid to look at her face, but try to break this habit as much as you can. You don't have to hold intense, loving contact the entire time you're talking to her or she may feel a little creeped out, but you should try to look into her eyes when she's talking as much as you can so she feels important. If you struggle to make eye contact or prefer to avoid it, try looking at her nose - but don't stare. Not everyone in the world can hold eye contact during conversation - tell her if you brave enough, a nice girl who is worth talking to will understand

Ask her questions. It's key to make the girl feel special as soon as you can. You can show her that you do really care about her by asking her questions, whether you're asking her about herself or about the things she's been up to recently. It doesn't have to be super personal -- and in fact, it shouldn't be -- but you should make an effort to show that you're trying to get to know her.[3] If she doesn't ask you anything back, then you can stay away from the questions for a while, or she may feel like she's being interrogated. Here are some things you can ask her about:

Her favorite hobbies and interests

Her favorite bands, books, or TV shows

Her favorite subjects in school

Her dream job

Her best friends

Her plans

Give her a compliment. Once you've talked for a bit, you can give the girl a small compliment to make her feel appreciated. You don't have to go overboard and shouldn't compliment her unless you really mean what you say. You can compliment her sweater, her new haircut, a piece of jewelry, or even an aspect of her personality. You shouldn't get too graphic ("You have great legs") or she'll get uncomfortable. Pick something PG and tell her that you like it to show that you care about her but don't want to overstep your bounds.[4]

Just one compliment per conversation is a good goal. You don't want her to feel like she's smothered with compliments, or like you don't really mean what you say.

Keeping Her Interested

1

Find common ground. Once you've gotten the conversation going, you can start to search for common ground so you and the girl can find something else to talk about. Though you don't actually have to have anything in common to have a great conversation, finding common ground can help you make a connection a bit more easily. When you talk to the girl, try to see if you can find something you share, whether it's a love for a certain sport or sports team, the fact that you grew up in the same place, or even a shared friend or teacher.

Talking about something you share can lead you to open up, see that you can have an exciting conversation, and to talk about new topics. For example, you can start by talking about how much you both love the 49ers, and then you can share your craziest stories about visiting their stadium, and from there, you may end up discussing your favorite things to do in San

Francisco, and so on.

Let the things you both share come up naturally instead of trying too hard to ask her if she likes the same things you do. Keep things open ended, so the conversation doesn't shut down if it turns out she doesn't share your interests. For example, instead of saying, "Did you see Frozen? That's my new favorite movie," you can say, "Have you seen anything interesting lately?

Ask for her opinion. This is another way to keep the conversation going and to show the girl that you really like talking to her and that she means something to you. If you ask for her opinion, from what she thinks about the current political situation to whether she likes your new shoes, she'll see that you see her as a human being and that you really value what she brings to the table. She'll see that you're not just trying to hit on her but actually care about her, and that you respect her as a person.

Don't ask her questions that can only be answered with a "yes" or a "no" and ask open-ended questions instead, so she has room to talk. Try "What do you think about..." instead of "Do you think that..."

Use your environment. If you're nervous and feel like the conversation is flagging, look around you and see if you can use your environment to your advantage. Maybe there's a flyer for a concert behind you and you can ask the girl if she likes the band. Maybe you're standing near a coffee shop and you can ask her if she ever goes there to read. Maybe you notice she's wearing a sweatshirt for a certain college that your sister went to and you can ask her about her connection to the school. Though you shouldn't start looking around distractedly the second you start the conversation, if you start running out of things to talk about, you can try to pick up some cues from what's around you.[6]

This is a creative way to keep the girl's interest and to keep her talking. She'll be impressed by how perceptive you are.

Make her laugh. If you want to keep the girl's interest, then cracking her up won't hurt. If you make the girl laugh, then she'll want to keep talking to you, so look for opportunities where you can put in a bit of humor. You can lightly poke fun at yourself, make fun of a person you both know in a kind way, or just tell her a corny joke if you really think she'll respond well. If you have a funny story that you think will actually make her laugh, you can tell it, as long as it's not too long and complicated. Don't overdo it, but look for opportunities to make the girl laugh.

If you're not naturally funny, then don't try so hard to be someone you're not. The girl will see that you're really making an effort and might feel bad for you. Instead, just work on being yourself, and if you can make the girl laugh in the process, then great.

If you don't know the girl very well, then don't tease her unless you're already flirting and teasing each other. She may take it the wrong way and can get offended, and you definitely don't want that.

Let her talk. You may be so nervous about not boring the girl that you could end up dominating the conversation so much that she can't get a word in. Talking the whole time does not mean that you are holding her interest; instead, pausing and leaving room for some silence can be a great opportunity for her to start saying something interesting, too. Don't put all of the pressure on yourself and make sure you are each talking about half of the time, or a little less or more if one of you is shy.

If you talk about yourself the whole time, then you'll look self-involved, and she won't want to keep talking to you.

Ask about her interests. Almost every girl loves talking about the things that mean the most to her, so don't forget to ask her about what she likes to do for fun, how often she does it, why she likes it, and why it means so much to her. You don't have to pry too much and you'll see that the girl's face lights up when she starts talking about something that is really important to her. This will make the girl feel special and like you really care about what makes her tick.

If she's not too elaborate when she discusses her interests, then you can share yours, as well.

Finishing Strong

Show her what makes you stand out. You don't have to do backflips to leave an impression. However, you do want to walk away from the conversation making the girl feel like she has gotten to know you a little bit and that she has a sense of what makes you stand out from all of the other guys out there. Maybe it's your sense of humor, your charm, or your love for the guitar. Whatever it is, let her in a little bit and show her who you really are. That way, when she sees you again, she'll have something to talk about and will have fond memories of your last conversation.

She doesn't have to know everything about you by the end of your ten or fifteen minute conversation. But she should walk away with at least one or two interesting facts about you. If you were just making small talk the whole time, then it would be hard to get to know each other on a real level.

Don't try too hard. Remember to stay relaxed and to be yourself and know that the girl is likely just as nervous as you are. This means that you don't have to tell wildly made-up stories to get her attention or to talk about something you don't really like, like motorcycles, just because you think it'll make you sound cool. You shouldn't curse or say bad things about people just because you think it'll catch her eye. Just take a deep breath, relax, and talk about the things that you would say to any friend of yours instead of putting on an extra performance for the girl.

If you're trying too hard, then the girl will be able to tell. Your goal should be to make her see that you like talking to her without showing that you think your conversation is a big deal.

Keep things positive. As you feel the conversation wrapping up, remember to stay positive, no matter what you're talking about. If you spent the last five minutes complaining about your parents, your teachers, the weather, or something else that has been getting you down, then the girl won't be left with a very positive impression. You want her to leave with good vibes and to remember that talking to you was actually fun, not annoying or even painful.[7]

You may feel like griping, and you can do it a little bit if you and the girl can bond over something that annoys both of you, but try to save your negative thoughts for someone who knows you a little better.

Keep your confidence up. Remember to stay confident throughout the conversation. Show the girl that you really believe in what you're saying and that you're happy to be who you are. If she gets this sense, then she'll see that you're a guy who is comfortable in his own skin and someone who is fun and easy to talk to. If you're nervous, putting yourself down, or making comments about how you can't find anything to talk about, then she'll feel uncomfortable and will be less likely to want to talk to you again.[8]

You don't need to act like you're the most interesting guy in the world or that you're hot enough to be a movie star; just act like you're happy with being you and the rest will follow.

There's a difference between bragging and being confident. If you brag too much, the girl will be turned off

Say goodbye while you're still having a good time. This is a great way to leave a positive impression. If you find that the conversation is going really well and that you're having a great time and have really clicked, then tell the girl you really like talking to her but that you have to go. Though it may seem ridiculous to leave in the middle of an amazing conversation, this is exactly when you should leave if you want to leave an unforgettable impression in her mind. If you wait too long, you may see that the conversation drags or that you have nothing to talk about, and why would she want to talk to you again after that? Wait until you've really hit it off and then tell her you have to go as nicely as you can.

If you're really feeling bold and the conversation has gone super well, you can even work up the courage to ask her to hang out again.

6 Things You Can Do To Cope With Boredom At A Time Of Social Distancing

More and more of us are staying home in an attempt to slow down the spreading coronavirus. But being stuck at home can lead to boredom.

Boredom is a signal that we're not meaningfully engaged with the world. It tells us to stop what we're doing, and do it better – or to do something else.

But, as a social psychologist who studies boredom, I know that people don't always make the best choices when bored. So if you're stuck at home, dutifully practicing your social distancing, how do you keep boredom away?

About boredom

We can feel bored even with jobs and activities that appear to be meaningful. For example, researchers have found anesthesiologists and air traffic controllers find themselves bored on the job.

What this research reveals is that just because something is objectively meaningful doesn't mean it feels that way to us all the time. And even meaningful work can be boring if the person performing it finds it too hard or too easy. Once that happens, individuals might struggle to stay focused.

Reducing boredom requires that individuals solve the problems that produced it – not having sufficient activities that are both meaningful and optimally challenging.

However, sometimes people turn to activities that make them feel better in the moment, but that don't provide long-term meaning or challenge. For instance, studies have shown that people are willing to self-administer electric shocks when bored.

Other behaviors linked to greater susceptibility to boredom include increased alcohol intake and marijuana use. Boredom is also tied to unhealthy snacking and online pornography.

While these may feel good in the moment, they provide only temporary relief from boredom. To prevent boredom and keep it away, we need to find solutions at home that provide lasting meaning and challenge.

1. Remind yourself why you're doing this

People generally prefer doing something to doing nothing. As staying home is the most effective way to prevent the further transmission of the coronavirus, it is meaningful to socially isolate. However, it may not always feel that way.

Like all emotions, boredom is about whatever you're thinking at the moment. That means staying at home will only feel meaningful when we're actively thinking about the greater good it does. For instance, in studies, when students were prompted to reflect on why their schoolwork mattered to them personally, researchers found that their interest in learning increased.

In other words, reframing our activity changes how we feel about it.

Creating simple reminders, such as a note on the fridge, or a morning meditation, can help us keep the big picture in view: Staying home is a sacrifice we're actively making for the good of others.

2. Find a rhythm

Routines structure our days, and provide a sense of coherence that bolsters our meaning in life. People's lives feel more meaningful in moments when they're engaged in daily routines.

We lose those routines when we give up going to the office, or when we are laid off. Even retirees or stay-at-home parents are disrupted by closures to cities, restaurants and schools. This loss of routine can foster feelings of boredom.

By creating new routines, people can restore a sense of meaning that buffers them from boredom.

3. Go with the flow

Figuring out what to do when faced by long days unstructured by work or school can be hard. A recent study of people in quarantine in Italy found that boredom was the second most common issue, after loss of freedom.

One thing that makes such situations hard is that it can be tricky to find activities that are just challenging enough to keep one occupied, without being too demanding. This situation can leave people bored and frustrated.

It helps to keep in mind that what counts as too challenging, or not challenging enough, will shift throughout the day. Don't force yourself to keep at it if you need a break.

4. Try something new

Boredom urges many of us towards the novel. Embrace that urge, judiciously. If you have the energy, try a new recipe, experiment with home repairs, learn a new dance on TikTok.

Doing new things not only relieves boredom, it helps acquire new skills and knowledge that may relieve boredom in the long run. For instance, we feel a surge of interest when we read an interesting novel or go through complex experiences, but only if we have the capacity to understand them.

Evidence shows that embracing new experiences, can help us lead not only a happy or meaningful life, but a psychologically richer one.

5. Make room for guilty pleasures

It's okay to binge on television, if that's all you can handle at the moment.

We sometimes paint ourselves into a box where our most meaningful hobbies are also mentally taxing or effortful. For instance, digging into a classic Russian novel may be meaningful, but it doesn't necessarily come easily.

Similarly, well-intentioned suggestions for how to cope at home, such as hosting a virtual wine-and-design night, may be simply too exhausting to be pleasurable at a time when many of us are already struggling.

Give yourself permission to enjoy your guilty pleasures. If need be, reframe those moments as much-needed mental refreshment, nourishing and recharging you for a later date.

6. Connect with others

Finding easy meaningful alternatives – bite-sized options that don't take much effort, but that we find deeply rewarding – can be a challenge.

Luckily one good option is open to us all: connecting with others, whether virtually or for those lucky enough not to be quarantined alone – in-person.

Create room for that virtually as well: Next time you're pouring a glass of wine or watering the plants, call up a friend while you do it. Make dinner together. We don't have to be bored, when we're all in this together.

www.ingramcontent.com/pod-product-compliance
Ingram Content Group UK Ltd.
Pitfield, Milton Keynes, MK11 3LW, UK
UKHW041830200726
13854UKWH00002BA/912